Jeep®

Jeep ®

David Fetherston

Motorbooks International
Publishers & Wholesalers ®

This edition first published in 1995 by Motorbooks International Publishers & Wholesalers, PO Box 2, 729 Prospect Avenue, Osceola, WI 54020 USA.

© Reed International Books 1995.
Reprinted Autumn 1996

Previously published by Osprey, an imprint of Reed Books, Michelin House, 81 Fulham Road, London, England.

Motorbooks International books are also available at discounts in bulk quantity for industrial or sales-promotion use. For details write to Special Sales Manager at the Publisher's address.

ISBN 0-7603-0184-0

Printed and bound in Hong Kong

Editor Shaun Barrington
Page design Paul Kime, The Black Spot

This book is dedicated to the American patriots and unsung heroes of American Bantam who designed and built, in the wink of an eye, the first Jeep: Karl K. Probst, Harold Crist, Chester Hempfling and Ralph Turner.

Acknowledgements

I would like to thank the owners of the Jeeps we photographed for their time and interest in helping us accomplish this project. Special thanks to: George Milne in Blairstown, Pennsylvania, for his time and use of historic Bantam photos; George E Domer in Milton, Pennsylvania, for his review of the text and Bantam photos; Lindsay Brooke for his review of the text; Ed Simmonds for his Australian WWII Jeep photos and stories; Bill Delaney and Pete Biro and their stunning images of Jeeps; Dr Steve Werlin, the heart-plumber; Mike Rose from the *Automobiles* TV series; Paul Barry of Cazadero, California, for his help with Jeep history, vehicles and photography. At Fetherston Publishing I would like to thank Nanette Simmons, with special thanks to Gloria for her editorial help in smoothing out the wrinkles in the text.

I want to thank the folks at Jeep/Chrysler: Lauri McTavish, Bob Kirkwood, Alex Tsigdinos, Alan Miller and Marci Greenfield along with Barbara Fronczak and Brandt Rosenbush at the Chrysler Historical Collection, without whose help I could never have completed this project.

Unless noted, the photography in this book was shot by me or provided by Jeep. My photos were taken with a Mamiya RB 6X7 Pros S camera system. It's a tough machine, just like a Jeep. Once again all the film was Fuji RDP 100, superbly processed by The Lab in Santa Rosa, California.

The TV series Rat Patrol *used a pair of .50 calibre machine gun-equipped MB's as part of the main story theme featuring actors Chris George (left) as Sgt Sam Troy and Larry Casey as Pvt Mark Hitchcock. The series centred around four commandos, Sam Troy, Mark 'Hitch' Hitchcock, Tully Pettigrew and Jack Moffitt who acted as: 'undisciplined mavericks, who wrote their own rules and conducted their own brand of warfare' against the Germans in the North African desert during the Second World War. Filmed in Spain, the ABC series first aired in colour on Mondays at 8:30 pm in 1966. The series became one of America's most popular weekly TV shows.*

Introduction

In the story of the 100 years' development of the automobile, one machine, the Jeep, has its own, particularly honourable chapter. During World War II it was a tremendous aid to the Allied Forces, helping them to achieve world peace during the desperate times when man's inhumanity knew no bounds.

The US Army's Quartermaster, since the beginning of the automobile, had been testing production vehicles and even issuing contracts for the development of a light reconnaissance vehicle. When the world found itself teetering once again on the brink of another major war, the need to have this type of vehicle became paramount.

Given only a few days to come up with the design, Karl K Probst and the crew at American Bantam Company took the mass of collected Army research into a dusty office and, working 18-hour days, subsequently delivered the first prototype, Bantam 'BRC', 49 days later.

Unfortunately, American Bantam did not get the opportunity to make its mark on military – and industrial – history with this fabulous little vehicle; other companies were given Bantam's design, who were in a better position to meet the Army's urgent production needs.

Barney Roos at Willys perfected the LRC into the Jeep and Ford, given Willys' blueprints, were contracted to do a production run. Boatloads were shipped to Britain and Africa to be used in the Allied battles and when the Japanese attacked Pearl Harbor in December 1941, the US Army had thousands of vehicles ready for service.

Upon historical review, it is recognized that the Jeep came from the clear and logical thinking of several groups of talented engineers and Army personnel. Their work produced one of the century's most significant automobiles. Without this rugged little buggy, the course of World War II may well have been very different.

Today, half a century later, we continue to use the Jeep in its many derivations for security, work and, of course, fun.

Contents

'The Sun Never Sets on the Mighty Jeep'

An inexpensive fast reconnaissance vehicle had been the US Army's dream for 30 years. As early as 1910 the Quartermaster Corps had called upon the 26th Infantry Division to test a series of Light Reconnaissance Vehicles or Scout Cars. Testing was done at Aberdeen Proving Grounds in Maryland, Camp Perry in Ohio, and Fort Riley, Kansas, and was based on production vehicles from a dozen American manufacturers. Nothing came close to satisfying their needs.

Two of the early participants were Ford and Hupmobile who supplied the Army with two-wheel-drive speedster style cars. These apparently did quite a good job but were far from the all-purpose off-roader they wanted.

Major L H Campbell oversaw the testing and later William Beasley and Captain Carl Terry stripped a Model T Ford and fitted it with aircraft balloon tires and chains for improved traction. It was a great idea and offered superior flexibility and traction to wheeled vehicles, but the

The Army had been experimenting for years to find the answer to its scout/reconnaissance car question. Early on, this 1911, 20 hp Hupmobile runabout was used at Fort Riley, Kansas, in an experiment with lightweight vehicles. Over the next 20 years the Army would test vehicles from a dozen different manufacturers. The driver and passenger are draped with a wet weather coverall to keep them and the interior dry and warm during inclement weather.

The Bantam was a 49-day wonder. Its birth was not so difficult as it was conceived in just three days based on Army requests and ideas for the ideal light reconnaissance vehicle. The creative engineering talents of Karl Probst, Harold Crist, Chester Hempfling and Ralph Turner were needed to design, build and test the first prototype. The body was hand-fabricated while the hood and the front fenders were scrounged from a local junk yard and modified to suit the car. (George E Domer, Photo Archives)

results did not match the Army's requirements. What the Army wanted was a vehicle to replace the horse and the motorcycle, to carry cargo and people, and traverse any type of ground. One design appeared for a motor cart with the driver walking behind. It was quickly abandoned but in the sixties this idea resurfaced as the 'Mule'.

During the First World War nearly 20,000 Model T Fords were pressed into service doing all kinds of military work. They did a fine job considering their primitive construction and two-wheel-drive.

In the mid-thirties the Army continued to test many light weight vehicles including vehicles from American Bantam Car Company, Ford and Chevrolet. They even tried to develop their own low cost, low profile, scout car. It was called the 'Belly Flopper' and was designed with a lay-down driving position so that it could achieve the smallest profile.

Designed by Captain Robert Howie and built by Master Sargent Melvin Wiley from the Fort Benning Infantry School, the Belly Flopper was less than 30 inches high and could crawl across the ground using vegetation for cover. It was not fast enough, however, or tough enough to take the pounding the Army testers inevitably put it through.

Roy Evans, owner of the American Bantam Car Comapny, was also interested in the scout car idea. To this end he lent the 112th Infantry, Pennsylvania National Guard, a pair of production American Bantam roadsters to use during their annual summer encampment in 1938. These stock 1,000 lb roadsters proved to be quite effective and drew favorable comments from the military test drivers for their agility and light weight.

The Marmon-Harrington company added a chapter to the scout car story by convincing the US Army of the advantages of a four-wheel drive with their conversions on Ford trucks, wagons and sedans. The Army tested these 4x4 vehicles at the King Ranch in Texas, tearing up the back country with the agility of mountain goats. The ½ ton truck

Above

After 48 days of 18-hour shifts, the engineering team at Bantam's Butler, Pennsylvania factory posed for this group photo. Harold Crist is seated in the driver's seat; Karl Probst is leaning on the spare wheel. Without the help of this hard working and creative group, Bantam would never have been able to design, get approved or build the first 'Jeep' in such a short time. Today, Detroit takes longer to design and prototype door handles for its new cars than this complete vehicle to took to produce. (George E Domer Photo Archives)

Right

The American Bantam Car Company facility in Butler, Pennsylvania, as it was in 1940. Francis Fenn, president of Bantam, seized the moment for the company when the Army offered them the opportunity to build a reconnaissance vehicle. He had the facility, the workers and most of the talent to build it. (George Milne Collection)

was apparently their favourite as they ordered 64 in 1939.

It was becoming apparent that America would have to join the war in Europe and unless the US military were well equipped, it could prove to be a disastrous endeavour. With the threat of war growing stronger every day the Army pressed ahead with its aim to obtain a task-built ¼ ton Light Reconnaissance Car (LRC).

The specifications were finally agreed upon at a meeting of the Ordinance Technical Committee on 27 June 1940. These specifications provided no design, only acute guidelines which had been arrived at during all the years of testing.

The basic list read like this:

- 1200 lb weight limit
- Four-wheel-drive
- Seating for three plus driver
- Simple tooled bodywork
- 3 mph crawling speed
- Minimum 50 mph top speed
- Folding windscreen
- Low speed cooling
- Grade climbing limits
- Machine gun pedestal mount, built into the chassis
- Six and a half inch min. ground clearance at axle center
- 75 inch maximum wheelbase
- 47 inch track
- Engine with at least 85 ft-lb of torque
- 600 lb payload
- Pilot car delivered in 49 days
- Running prototypes in 75 days

The Axis victories in Europe and Asia were being monitored by the American government but the military were more aware of the possible forthcoming battles. The Army knew they would need the LRC on hand and sent 135 Letters of Intent to auto manufacturers expressing their desire for the company to put forward a proposition.

A stipulation of the 70-vehicle $175,000 contract was that a single running prototype had to be delivered within 49 days. This seemingly impossible task turned away many bidders and only two companies replied, American Bantam and Willys-Overland. American Bantam was the sole contractor prepared to deliver a pilot model within the time limit. Willys-Overland wanted more time and the Army agreed.

This is the chassis of the first Bantam prototype showing the Continental engine and Spicer four-wheel-drive system. It was extraordinarily simple and very flexible using only two cross members. (George Milne Collection)

Other factors were also at work. American Bantam was in severe financial straits and the offer of $175,000 was very tempting. But their design office had been closed for a time and the company consisted of a handful of staff at the plant in Butler, Pennsylvania. Company owner, Evans, and President Francis Fenn, considered the daunting task of finding an engineer at short notice who could work capably and quickly enough to finalize a design for a completely new automobile within a finite time.

Karl K Probst, a graduate of Ohio State University in Mechanical Engineering, was recommended. Probst had studied gear design in France and had worked on a secret light car project for Ford. He owned the PSM Design Studio in Detroit and did creative and engineering work for numerous Detroit auto makers.

Karl was reluctant at first to work with Bantam due to its financial status and the problem of having only a few days to come up with a design. However, the challenge stimulated him. He was informed that Bantam employees Harold Crist and Chester Hempfling would be working with him and that he would use existing production Bantam car parts where possible.

Karl dropped everything, packed a bag and headed for Butler, Pennsylvania, via Toledo, Ohio. In Toledo he visited Bob Lewis, Chief Engineer at Spicer. They assembled a pair of axles, a transfer case and drive shaft assemblies. Spicer had a suitable front axle and the rear was obtained by narrowing a production Studebaker Champion unit.

Every kind of hazard was tested by Captain Mosely. The Bantam prototype is seen here ploughing through the mud and water course at the Holabird testing ground. The little 4x4 was pounded day and night until it broke. The Army were impressed but still not sure that the Bantam was up to the job. (George E Domer Photo Archives)

Karl then drove to Butler, Pennsylvania, and the next morning he met with Francis Fenn and Harold Crist. Within an hour Karl and Crist were rolling up their sleeves and dusting off the drawing boards.

The only guidelines the team were given were a list of specifications and a simple drawing of a four-passenger, open scout car. Probst toured the warehouse at Bantam looking for pre-existing production components he could use.

Over the next three days Karl drafted out the first Bantam LRV scout car. Although it did not meet the Quartermaster's 1,275 lb weight limit, all the basic design elements and style were set for the new design. Once Karl had his specifications laid out, the physical dimensions of the body fell into place. The body was made using simple flat panels to speed production with round or square tube where possible. The Bantam engine was discarded early in the project as it produced insufficient horsepower. A Continental Model BY4112 (45 hp at 3,500 rpm) industrial flathead engine took its place.

The rounded nose on the first 70 Bantams was one of the few major design variations to the final Jeep design and 50 years later it's easy to see that the design's brilliance lay in its simplicity and functional elegance. Karl had the design and costing work completed by Sunday morning. He blueprinted the designs, then helped Fenn complete the necessary paperwork for the contract bid application. By noon on Sunday they were headed for Baltimore to seek contractual approval. (Just think about that for a moment: costings by noon?)

They met with the military's Purchasing and Contracting Office along with Ford and Willys representatives. Within an hour Bantam had been awarded the contract, on the basis of being able to deliver a vehicle within the contract's 49 day limit.

The Willys Quad was delivered to the Army two months after Bantam had delivered their testing prototype in September of 1940. Two versions were delivered, one with four-wheel-steering. Probst and Bantam were not pleased at the new Willys Quad. They screamed 'infringement of design'. The Army and the courts later settled that fight mostly in Bantam's favour.

As the Army wanted a variety of models they asked Willys and Ford to continue to develop their designs. The Purchasing and Contracting office were unsure if Bantam could deliver the vehicle in the quantities that would be needed. Willys and Ford were given immediate access to Bantam blueprints and were allowed to attend Bantam's upcoming testing. Barney Roos, chief engineer at Willys, persuaded his management board to fund two pilot vehicles. He was well aware of what it would mean to Willys if they got the contract to build thousands of vehicles for the Army.

At Bantam, Harold Crist, Chester Hempfling and Ralph Turner, along with a handful of mechanics and fabricators, commenced building the first pilot model. They worked 49 days and nights to accomplish their daunting task.

Body panels were fabricated from raw stock or sourced from local junk yards and converted to fit. Brackets and supports were hand-fabricated and the single pilot model was readied for quick testing at

Bantam. No major deficiencies were found and the little Bantam performed hill-climbing feats which challenged even their own optimistic pre-conceptions.

The pilot vehicle was driven to the Army's Camp Holabird testing range in Maryland with Karl Probst and Harold Crist taking turns at the wheel. This 230 mile trip had a multifold effect: not only did it break in the drivetrain and engine, it gave them a chance to see how the new car would perform and what kind of gas mileage it would achieve. It also delivered the Bantam to the Army within half an hour of the contract's deadline on 23 September 1940.

Testing took place immediately. Representatives from Willys-Overland and Ford were on hand and the Bantam performed extremely well in its initial testing. Over the next three weeks it was pounded unmercifully by Captain Mosley and his crew until it finally broke. By

Above

This was the second Willys prototype the 'MA'. Barney Roos designed and built it to meet the Quartermasters Corps' contract specifications for an LRV or scout car. It featured a flat hood and grille which gave it a different look up front to the Bantam.

Left

This wonderfully restored 1940 Bantam BRC was built as part of the first batch of 1,500 that the Army ordered. Powered by a 40 hp Continental four-cylinder engine which drove a full Spicer four-wheel-drive system. The Bantam proved to be a wonderfully agile, go-anywhere vehicle. Seen here with the top or 'tilt' up, the Bantam features grab handles, canvas doors, open cutaway front fenders and dished recesses in the front fenders for the headlights. Owner: George Milne.

then the Army testers were fully convinced that the concept was right on track.

The Quartermaster Corps and the military's Purchasing and Contracting office liked what they saw but considered it was still over-weight, under-powered and in need of more rugged construction. Barney Roos delivered Willys' 'Quad' prototype on 13 November 1940 and Ford's GP version followed later that month. Much to Bantam's indignation the vehicles looked like shadows of their design. But the Willys was more powerful and heavier in construction and Ford's, although similar, was powered by a Ford tractor engine. Access to Bantam's blueprints and specifications had made this project very simple for the two manufacturing giants and both Bantam and Probst were

Above

The Bantam BRC featured a full height top which could be folded or removed. It rolled along on 15-inch steel wheels capped with Atlas tyres (Firestones originally). The spare was carried mounted to the rear of the vehicle. This was the second generation of the Bantam and incorporated many changes from the original prototype. However, even with these running changes, Bantam delivered a batch of 70 BRC's to the Army by December of 1940. Owner: George Milne.

Right

The interior of the Bantam BRC was as basic as was needed to operate the vehicle. A steering wheel, clutch, brake and throttle pedals, and a pair of pressed steel canvas-covered bucket seats were up front with a small full-width bench seat in the rear. The instruments were from a Bantam automobile and a set of brass 'Vehicle Operation' plates were attached to the dash. Owner: George Milne.

Above

Under the hood of the Bantam BRC is a 40 hp Continental Model BY4112 four-cylinder engine. Bantam had a lightweight four-cylinder of their own, but right from the start of the project it was deemed under-powered and the Continental was used instead. Owner: George Milne.

Above right

The Quartermaster also tested the Ford GP as severely as it had the Bantam and the Willys. It was pounded day and night at Camp Holabird in Maryland. Production started in February 1941 and the GP is seen here being tested with the prototype Willys MA following. The Ford GP still differed from the Willys substantially but that changed in November 1941 when the Standard Jeep was adopted, which employed design elements of all three prototypes.

Right

Once the testing of the Bantam BRC-40's were completed, some of the first batch of 1,500 were handed over for training purposes. Here an MP traverses a creek in mid-1941 after several enlisted men had cleared a log from his path. Tougher challenges were yet to come. (George Milne Collection)

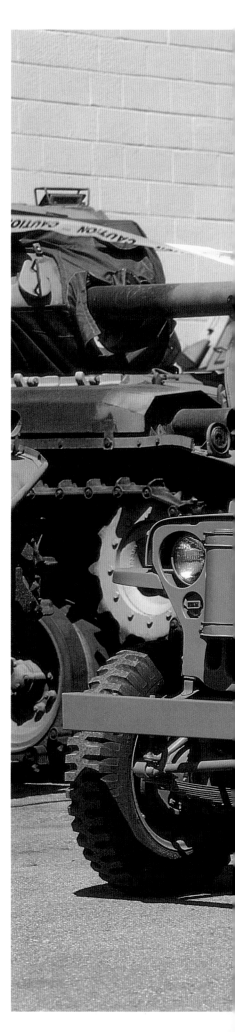

mortified at the resemblance. But the Quartermaster claimed the design work belonged to the Army and the Army could do whatever they wanted with it.

Roos had been developing a Whippet design into the new four cylinder 'Go-Devil' engine for Willys Americar line and immediately knew it would be the right engine for his 'Quad'. He also knew that he could get a complete four-wheel-drive system from parts which Bantam had already paid Spicer to engineer for the project.

Bantam further refined their vehicle. The Willys Quad and Ford GP underwent successful 5,000 mile testing runs. Bantam and Willys had always known that the Quartermaster's specified weight for the vehicle was way off base and eventually, after much negotiation and

Above

This 'Saturday night special' was an officially released military photo. Interestingly, troops were generally not allowed or encouraged to use any military vehicles for such pleasures. The young lady was handing out Cokes to the three neatly dressed men on board this Bantam BRC. Note the incorrect passenger car front tyre on the driver's side and the interesting offering of 'Fried Chicken Livers and Gizzards' on the Cafe's menu. (George Milne Collection)

Right

By 1942 the BRC-40, the Quad, the MA and the Pygmy had lost their entities with the mass production of the standardized GPW and MB Jeeps. This 1942 Ford-built GPW was built with the Willys-designed 'Go-Devil' engine, not the Fordson tractor engine which had been used in the early Ford GP's. It has been restored with Shore Patrol livery and suitable dull grey paint. Owner: David Mangold.

demonstration, the weight limit was raised to 2,100 lb. Apparently the turning point to this problem came during testing of the Bantam when three burly enlisted men at the proving ground walked over to the vehicle and lifted the rear end clear off the ground!

Before the Willys was fully tested the Quartermaster's Office brought Bantam, Willys and Ford into a meeting to inform them that in March, 1941, they would contract each of them to build 1,500 vehicles.

Bantam was the first to deliver 1,175 production models. Many of these were shipped under a Lend-Lease agreement to Russia and Britain. Within months all three manufacturers had production vehicles on the test course at the Camp Holabird Quartermaster Depot in Baltimore, Maryland. The Willys version proved to be the significant player with its rugged construction and higher horsepower and thus the Willys MA was selected as the basic version.

The Quartermaster Corps had figured that American Bantam did not have the manufacturing potential to cover a project where possibly hundreds of thousands of vehicle were involved. However, as in all War Games, behind the decisions was a mass of political intrigue as one company played its senators and supporters off against the Secretary of War, Henry Stimson. Bantam continued building its version and eventually delivered 2,675 production models by the end of 1941.

The Army now looked to Willys with their newly refined design, rugged construction and improved power to develop the model. Bids were called once again and Willys offered the lowest.

Barney Roos set to refining his 'MA' into the 'MB'. He had to get its weight down to 2,100 lb which meant shaving nearly 300 lb off the MA prototype's weight. He did this by carefully examining every part and eliminating or cutting away unessential material.

Willys quickly evolved the MB as 'The Standardized Jeep' incorporating Ford's design for a stamped metal grille with recessed headlamps. It was easily fabricated with shallow-draw body panels and now met the weight limit by ounces. It featured additions of axe and spade mounts, blackout lights, machine gun mounts on some models, increased fuel tank capacity, a five-gallon jerrycan mounted at the rear and a centre-mounted emergency brake.

The new contract called for 16,000 MB model Jeeps but the Army wanted a second source of supply. Ford were asked to bid but the bid had to be based on Ford building a vehicle in which every part was completely interchangeable between the Ford and the Willys.

This meant that Ford would have to discard their tractor-engined GP 'Pygmy' used in the first production run and replace it with the standardized Willys MB. Willys agreed to this arrangement and did it with-

The tropics were as tough to deal with as the deserts. Because of the severe wet season simple methods of creating roads were devised, as can be seen with this Jeep traversing a log road made of coconut palm trunks at Merauke in Dutch New Guinea. Log roads were a simple engineering idea and were easily built using locally available materials. The track of this Jeep matches the lay of the dual log runners in this road/bridge. It was also in this area that "The Driver-less Jeep" became a legend. According to Ed Simmonds, author of Radar Yarns: 'The road to the radar station was so deeply rutted that the grooves acted like streetcar tracks and with the hand throttle set in the Jeep it could be sent along the road without a driver. Then the sender would call ahead to let them know it was coming.' (Frank Bound/Ed Simmonds Photo Archives)

Below

There were many and varied ideas used to carry stretcher patients in Jeeps. Some used two layers and carried up to seven patients. This arrangement worked out quite well with little adaptation needed to convert the Jeep for this use. This Willys carried three stretcher cases, one walking-wounded, a male nurse, an armed soldier and a driver to a field hospital in southern New Guinea in January 1943. (G Silk, Australian War Museum Photo Collection-014013)

out charge, turning over their production drawings and specifications to Ford who immediately picked the project up as the GPW-GP Willys.

At this time the pressed steel grille with recessed headlamps became the standard front end treatment. This came about because Ford engineers had designed the headlights to pivot back and light up the engine bay by mounting them on hinges.

With technical matters well taken care of Ford had little development work to do, only fabricate the tooling and start building, although the Ford was slightly different from the Willys. However, none of these pieces interfered with the interchangeability the Army wanted with the production vehicles.

Ford's only special engineering contribution was a run of 49 four-wheel-steering GPWs. Bantam also built a run of eight four-wheel-steering models but nothing came of this idea in production. Ford structured its chassis along the same design as Willys but built it out of a double U-channel, which was welded and formed so as to create a box-

section chassis which was at least as good as the original. As soon as the standardized Jeep had been formatted, serious production began and between 1941 and 1945 over 640,000 were built by Willys and Ford. Many innovative ideas were added to the basic vehicle. Winches were developed for the front of some, as were 'A' frame tow hitches designed not only for hauling the Jeep behind a large transporter but also for hooking two Jeeps together to form a tug to pull large artillery pieces like Howitzer cannons.

A six-wheeled version and a four-wheel-steering model were also developed but never went much beyond the prototype stage, or were only built in very small numbers.

The American Bantam Car Company did not get the contract to mass produce the Jeep. Francis Fenn at the American Bantam Car Company was disheartened as were Harold Crist, Karl Probst, Roy Evans and other Bantam employees who had worked so hard to make their BRC a reality.

However, Bantam did not collapse because it didn't get the contract but actually flourished by accepting other military work. They built floating Jeep cargo trailers by the thousands, torpedo motors and hydraulic control and landing gear equipment for aircraft, winning 'E' awards for their good work.

Willys and the Army continued to refine the Jeep with a waterproofing kit which allowed the vehicle to cross creeks and rivers up to two feet deep. They then developed a kit which would make a Jeep waterproof so that it could be completely submerged in water up to four feet. Several flotation systems were also developed for the Jeep.

A system for crossing ravines and rivers, on a pair of wire cables,

Many names had been tagged to the vehicle by this time: Quad, Buggy, Blitz Buggy, Peep, Midget, but the name 'Jeep' finally stuck for everyday usage. The origin of the name Jeep has a half-a-dozen sources including: a tough little character called 'Jeep' in a Popeye cartoon about the 'Land of the Jeeps'; a misunderstanding of the GP name tag by a *Washington Daily News* journalist who noted the GP as a jeep in her story; or it was picked up from the 'Jeep' tractor-trucks built by the Minneapolis-Moline Power Implement Company.

Interestingly the GP tag did not mean General Purpose, as has been long thought. The 'G' was a prefix for Government and the 'P' was the designation for an 80-inch wheelbase Reconnaissance Car. No-one seems to have the 'real' answer to how the name Jeep was attached to the vehicle.

was also devised using drums which bolted on the wheels. This allowed the Jeep to run on the cables stretched across a river or ravine as though it were crossing a solid bridge.

During the war the Jeep was used by every division of the US military. The Army, Navy and Air Force all had their specific uses for it. They were shipped in large numbers to the Allied Forces of Canada, Britain, Australia and New Zealand. The Jeep was used in every theatre of war from the depths of the Russian winter to the rains of Europe, the heat of the Pacific and dust of North Africa.

In the field Jeeps became a vital part of every land action. They were used to lay telephone communications, to transport the wounded, as taxis to carry battle commanders, generals, prime ministers and presidents. The Air Force delivered aircraft crew in them and they were modified for pulling railway cars. The Navy converted them for Shore Patrol duties and British commandos used them for high speed surprise raids on Rommel's forces in the North African desert. Apart from the Model T Ford, no other vehicle has ever been as beneficial in its usefulness, exceeding all expectations.

GIVIN' 'EM HELL AT GUADALCANAL

IN JEEPS FROM WILLYS-OVERLAND

THEY'RE doing it in the Solomons, too. Tough, tiger-like Marines and Army men, mounted in their fast, power-packed Jeeps built by Willys-Overland, are showing the fanatical Japs how FREE AMERICANS fight with modern American equipment.

Jeeps driven by the Willys-designed "Go-Devil" engine carried these great fighters when they crashed the shores of Guadalcanal. And Jeeps are carrying them *now*—in spite of hell or

high water or anything the Japs can do—carrying them swiftly and safely where no other four-wheeled fighting vehicle in *any* army in the world could take them.

This swift, shifty, and amazingly durable Army Jeep of ours is an American invention—created here—built here for our own army, marines and sailor men and for our Allies. Today it is unquestionably the most spectacular automotive fighting machine on every fighting front in the world, and

in training camps in America, Britain, Australi Alaska, Iceland and elsewhere.

Willys-Overland's civilian engineers assiste the U. S. Quartermaster Corps in designing ar perfecting the Jeep adopted by the U. S. Arm The amazing world-renowned "Go-Devil" engi that drives it with such power, speed, ar flexibility, is an exclusive Willys-Overland d velopment.

WILLYS-OVERLAND MOTORS, INC.

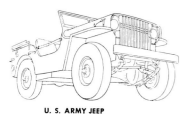

U. S. ARMY JEEP

WILLYS

MOTOR CARS   TRUCKS AND JEEPS

AMERICAR—the People's Car

THE GO-DEVIL ENGINE—power-heart of WILLYS CARS and all JEEPS

Left

'Givin' em Hell at Guadalcanal' is one of a series of Willys ads used during 1943. It uses not only heavily patriotic themes but reminds the reader that Willys is helping to win the war 'on every fighting front'. This rather improbable water-colour shows a Jeep mounted with a machine gun shooting down a Zero fighter at Guadalcanal with the help of a mobile searchlight. These wonderful paintings were done by the famous water-colourist James Sessions (1882-1964) as a private commission for Willys during the war. The series continued until post-war times when Sessions did another series of Willys paintings illustrating how useful the Jeep would be in a peacetime world.

Above

This was one of the 80,641 GPW's Ford built in 1943. This model served extensively on all battlefields from the Pacific to Europe and North Africa. It is restored as a close support and reconnaissance Jeep with a .50-calibre Browning machine gun, camouflage netting, field 'phone, water bags, hand tools, siren and accessories. Owner: A Burghardt.

War correspondent Ernie Pyle summed up the Jeep this way: 'It's as faithful as a dog, as strong as a mule and as agile as a goat.' Others sung its praises too. General Dwight Eisenhower, Allied Supreme Commander in Europe, referred to it proudly in a speech, after the war. 'The Jeep, the Dakota airplane, and the landing craft were the three tools that won the war.'

Above

The interior of this 1943 Ford GPW features many correct period accessories. These include a Springfield rifle, gas mask, helmet, field phone and brass fire extinguisher. Owner: A Burghardt

Right

New Guinea was a primitive country with few roads. The battles were fought in many cases by foot soldiers who slogged over the Owen Stanley Ranges. On the coast margins, road traffic found it tough going during the wet season when the roads turned to quagmires from the churning of four- and six-wheel-drive vehicles hauling loads over roads which were ill-constructed to carry such weight. Here a Jeep extracts another Jeep from a mud hole on the Godowa-Butawa Creek Road in southern New Guinea in December 1943. (Australian War Museum Photo Collection-061633)

The Sun Never Sets On the Mighty "J...

"JEEPS"... DESTINATION NETTUNO!

A tribute to our experts in Logistics

"JEEP" FUTURES

People all over the world are thinking of scout cars—"Jeeps" —made by *Willys*—of how they can be adapted to domestic uses after the war. A soldier in Alaska may be thinking at this moment— "When I get back I'll get a 'Jeep'. It'll make a swell delivery car."

A farmer boy home on a furlough thinks—"A 'Jeep' (scout car made by *Willys*) can beat a team of horses all hollow." And so it goes.

High school kids who see these scout cars—"Jeeps" made by *Willys*—in magazines and on the screen, are thinking of—"Gee, wouldn't it be swell to have a 'Jeep' at the lake after the war?" Are you "Jeep"-planning, too?

It is upon those hard working fellows skilled in the science of supply, known as "logistics", that our invasion forces depend for "the right things at the right time at the right place". And that includes plenty of tough, versatile "Jeeps".

Like ships, food, tanks, guns, ammunition and other vital material, the Willys scout car, known the world over as the "Jeep", is equipment used in Allied invasions. This was proved at Casablanca. It was true at Sicily and at Salerno. Likewise, in the daring - invasion of Italian beaches above Anzio, weather-grayed transports carried many rugged little "Jeeps" with "Destination Nettuno" understood, if not so labeled.

The Willys scout car means *mobility* for our invasion troops. *Speed* to carry men, materials, first aid, munitions—anywhere, any time. *Power* to pack guns or wounded men, or *anything*, through deep mud or over rocky mountain passes. And *dependable performance* to guarantee completed missions.

Yet, even today, as thousands of these Willys motorized units are serving our fighting forces in Italy and on other blazing battle fronts, soldiers who live and work with the mighty "Jeep", and civilians, too, are dreaming of it in terms of *after the war*.

They see this Willys scout car adapted to civilian use, and powered with its exclusive war-proved Willys Go-Devil "Jeep" Engine, applying its famous "Jeep" power, "Jeep" speed, "Jeep" versatility, dependability and economy to a wide variety of jobs in cities and towns, in business and industry, and on farms the world over.

Willys-Overland Motors, Inc., Toledo, Ohio

The power and stamina of the versatile "Jeep" will serve many needs in the years of reconstruction ahead.

WILLYS *Builds the Mighty* 'JEEP'

Left

'Jeeps... Destination Nettuno!' *This Jeep advertisement was published in 1944. It illustrated the daring invasion of Anzio, Italy, by an off-shore delivery of men and machines using landing craft to mount the storming of the beaches. The painting is underlined with the words 'The Sun Never Sets On the Mighty Jeep'. By 1944 Willys-Overland Motors Inc. were calling the Jeep their own with ads like this one. The ad also forecast the future with 'Jeep Futures', telling the reader that when the war was over Jeeps would see domestic use, on the farm, as a delivery truck and for fun.*

Above

This restored 1944 Willys MB, finished in its correct Olive Drab, is fitted out as a 44th Signal Battalion-5th Air Force Signal Corps wagon. It features a pair of BC 60 radios with canvas water proofing covers, spring mounted 'whip' antenna and a Surge Kit or Desert Cooling Tank mounted on the grille frame. Powered by the now-famous 'Go-Devil' four banger, the MB rolls along on non-directional tires and carries the correct axe and shovel as side mounts. Owner: David Young.

Above

In many ways the Jeep was a mechanic's dream. It was simple, easily serviced and compact. When work was needed underneath, the vehicle could be man-handled onto its side, exposing all the running gear. Seen here working on the four-wheel-drive system of this Jeep are R F Duncan and L W Powell, mechanics with the 231st Light Aid Detachment base in early 1944 on the Dallman River in New Guinea. (Australian War Museum Photo Collection-070660)

Right

The Jeep led an amazing life throughout the Second World War. It was crated and freighted, broken down and built up, modified, converted and moved about by sea, rail, road and air. This photo, taken at Ward's Drome in Port Moresby, Papua New Guinea, in early 1944, shows Lt Underwood from the 54th US Troop Carrier Group (Indianapolis, Indiana) instructing Australian and American transport crew on how to load a complete Jeep into a C-47. This aircraft was wing-less and motor-less and was used just for practice loading of Jeeps and equipment. By this stage of the war the Jeep had become a front-line fighting vehicle and it was imperative that they be easily and rapidly deployed where they were most needed. (Australian War Museum Photo Collection-070533)

The Ford GPW came in a number of configurations and was optioned or converted to different uses during its operational life. This interestingly restored 1945 GPW features an original capstan winch, tow bar, Springfield rifle and surge tank. The tow bar was a triangulated design offering high strength. It allowed two or more Jeeps to be hitched together to pull artillery or other heavy cargo including rail cars. Attached is an original Bantam-built amphibious trailer designed to float, loaded with 500 lb. The trailer was also designed to interchange springs and wheels with the Jeep and featured its own handbrake and hitch stand. Owner: Gary Schultz.

S 1731-2

Post-World War II

The Jeep featured in dozens of fictional and documentary movies during the forties and fifties. Here, Glenn Ford blasts onto the set of the 1958 MGM movie Imitation General. *This comedy-drama, set in France in 1944, revolves around a Sergeant who takes command to keep up morale after his General is killed in action. Directed by William Hawks, it also starred Red Buttons.*

As time, fate, and the courts would have it, the American Bantam company never fulfilled its destiny to build the production series Jeep.

With the cessation of hostilities, Ford immediately abandoned its Jeep GPW production line and returned to building civilian automobiles. It was a different matter at Willys. They had already civilianized the MB, hoping to sell it to returning troops who knew the Jeep's abilities.

It seemed like a good plan but fighting a war with a purpose-built vehicle was a far cry from commuting to New York in one. In 1944-45 Willys nifty ads stated: 'The Sun Never Sets on the Mighty Jeep' and they focused their sales on attracting farmers, not commuters, to an all-purpose vehicle to power their farm implements, run to town, and haul small loads.

During this time the American Bantam Company took Willys to court and won a rather hollow victory. After several years of investigation the Federal Trade Commission eventually assigned American Bantam Company the title of originator and developer of the Jeep but gave Willys the right to use the name and to build the vehicle after a second trade name court battle between Bantam and the Minneapolis-Moline Power Implement Company.

In retrospect, Barney Roos at Willys-Overland did contribute a great deal to the Jeep as a refined fighting machine. He took the concept and made it into a reliable, life saving, battle winning scout car based on Bantam's design.

It was Roos who could sense the end of WW II and it was he who initiated the post-war versions of the MB Jeep. He envisaged a massive market for an agricultural version and commissioned 22 prototypes, code-named CJ-1A. The CJ designation was for 'Civilian Jeep' and the production models which emerged from Willys in August, 1945, were MB versions which included a tailgate, side-mounted spare, larger headlamps and an external fuel cap. It was introduced as the CJ-2A and sold for $1,090. The new all-steel station wagons appeared from Willys in September 1946. For Jeep it was a forecast of the future, the forerunner to the modern Jeep Cherokee 28 years later.

The station wagon was one of the first all-new automobiles after WW II. Barney Roos had commissioned Brooks Stevens to design a new product line-up. Willys' President, Sorenson, specified that the new vehicle would have to use the Jeep's front sheet metal and 104-inch wheelbase chassis.

Within a year it was available as a sedan delivery truck and station wagon. Combinations of two- and four-wheel-drive would become available in these models along with the 148 cubic-inch 'Lightning' six-cylinder engine. Development of the CJ Jeep continued and in 1949 the CJ-3A which featured a one-piece windshield, was introduced.

Within a short time Brooks Stevens had convinced Willys to build a sporty Jeep. Known as the VJ2, the new 'Jeepster' began production in

t's a Power-House on Wheels

The 4-Wheel-Drive 'Jeep' handles jobs that stump ordinary vehicles

DOUBLE - BARRELED POWER—that's the Universal "Jeep." It has the power to reach the job, then furnishes power from its own "Jeep" Engine to operate auxiliary equipment, such as this 200 amp welder-generator, carried in the "Jeep." Power take-off is also used for compressors and sprayers.

EYOND THE ROAD'S END, where the going is rough and steep, you can depend on the sure-ooted, 4-wheel-drive pulling power of the Universal "Jeep" to take a load through. With a Jeep," you can climb steep grades, maneuver your way in dense woods, traverse loose rock nd sand—*and get there!* That's why the Universal "Jeep" has become essential equipment for ngineers, surveyors, geologists, ranchers, miners and lumber men.

HUB - DEEP IN THE MUD of a construction site, this Universal "Jeep" pulled itself out when a shift to 4-wheel drive added the tractive power of "live" front wheels. "Jeep" all-wheel traction is a life-saver, too, when snow and ice cover the road.

● The 4-wheel-drive Universal "Jeep" is designed to do the "impossible" jobs that stop conventional vehicles. It is a versatile tool, rugged in construction, highly maneuverable, with a range of 6 speeds forward and 2 reverse. Ask your Willys-Overland dealer for a demonstration of this many-purpose vehicle built by the world's largest maker of 4-wheel-drive vehicles.

The 4-Wheel-Drive UNIVERSAL `Jeep´

WILLYS-OVERLAND MOTORS—MAKERS OF AMERICA'S MOST USEFUL VEHICLES

April, 1948, powered by the same ex-Whippet 134 cubic-inch, four-cylinder L-headed engine which had been developed into the 'Go-Devil'. Production carried over until 1951 with four and six-cylinder versions in two-wheel-drive only. The 1951 Jeepsters ended up being leftover 1950 models with new titles. Total Jeepster production for the four years amounted to about 19,000 units.

Above

In an effort to capitalize on their success with the Jeep Willys introduced a new line up of all-steel station wagons in 1946, and a panel delivery and pickup truck in 1947. The truck version was based on a 118-inch wheelbase chassis, it was offered in both two and four-wheel-drive, powered by the 63 hp 'Go Devil'. This 1947 Glenwood Green metallic truck is fitted with the factory truck bed, complete with side-mounted spare and was recently restored by its owner Paul Barry.

Right

The first 'compact' all-steel production station wagon was a Willys product offered in 1946. Interestingly, it looked like a woody wagon with pressed steel framing and three-tone paintwork which simulated the woody-look. It used Jeep running gear and MB-style front sheet metal and was designed to compete against the 'real' wood wagons still being built by Detroit's Big Three. The Station Wagon came in two-wheel-drive at first, then a four-wheel-drive version was offered in 1949. It carried through to 1963 virtually unchanged apart from a new six-cylinder engine.

The Car that gives you More for your Money:

A Roomy, Comfortable Passenger Car...

It's a sedan—with ample room for six people, plus luggage space for all the family. You'll like this nimble car's quick get-away, fast steering response ... short turning radius ... and wide-range, deep windows all around.

MORE MILEAGE AND LESS UPKEEP

The famous 'Jeep' Engine with fuel-stretching overdrive gives mileage that saves you money. You'll appreciate, too, the fine maintenance service you get from Willys-Overland dealers, and the low cost of parts and repairs.

...and a Utility Vehicle, too

The 'Jeep' Station Wagon gives you the extra value of double usefulness. Seats are easily removable to provide space for hauling bulky loads. See a Willys-Overland dealer for the car that delivers more for your money!

'Jeep'
Station Wagon

A REALLY NEW KIND OF CAR...

The 'Jeep' Station Sedan combines the luxurious riding ease of a sedan with the spaciousness of a station-wagon. Its finely appointed interior gives passengers extraordinary headroom and legroom. Its 6-cylinder engine, with overdrive, assures top performance and long fuel mileage.

Jeep Station Sedan

WILLYS-OVERLAND MOTORS, TOLEDO 1, OHIO • MAKERS OF AMERICA'S MOST USEFUL VEHICLES

Above

To complement the Station Wagon, Willys also produced a commercial Panel Delivery version. Available in two and four-wheel drive, the all-steel panel truck offered an enormous interior space with wide opening rear doors, making it suitable for every kind of commercial use, from laundry delivery to painters and electricians and as a general-purpose commercial wagon. Powered by an F-headed six-cylinder engine, this 1951 Potomac Grey and Surf Grey metallic Panel Delivery belongs to Paul Barry who specializes in the restoration of vintage Jeeps in Cazadero, Sonoma County, California.

Left

Willys-Overland built over 10,000 of the first VJ2 Jeepster in 1948. It was on the expensive side for new cars, with a $1,886 price tag, but was priced about the same as a new Ford convertible at the time. Power was delivered from an ex-Whippet four-cylinder engine which Barney Roos had re-engineered into the successful 'Go-Devil', L-headed four-cylinder engine. The Jeepster body styling was an original idea of Brooks Stevens, the famous industrial designer who sold the idea of using existing chassis and front sheet metal to create a sporty roadster to the Company President Charles Sorensen. This original example of a Slate Grey/Black 1948 Jeepster is still driven daily by Paul Barry.

Above

The new Jeepster was the brainchild of Brooks Stevens, who added a sporty body and image to the Jeep line up with a fairly brilliant adaptation of Station Wagon running gear and sheet metal to a simple phaeton body change.

Left

The Jeepster changed very little during its short production life from 1948 to 1951. Based on the all-steel station wagon running gear and front sheet metal, it changed along with the wagon when it was uprated with new grille and engines. This 1951 Fiesta Yellow and Black Jeepster is powered by the F-headed, 72 hp 'Hurricane' four-cylinder engine. It is still in regular use by its second owner after having been purchased a few years ago from the owner of the old Willys Jeep dealership in Monte Rio, California. Owner: John Sasso.

The Fifties

In 1950 the truck line was revised with a new 72 hp 'Hurricane' high-compression four-cylinder, F-headed engine along with a new 'V-nosed' grille, fenders and hood. This new sheet metal would carry through until the series ended in 1962.

A second six-cylinder engine was also introduced in 1950. Known as the 'Hurricane', this 90 hp, F-headed engine was initially only available in the two-wheel-drive wagon or Jeepster. Interestingly, the Station Wagon was built by Willys Overland in Brazil and the design was licensed out to Mitsubishi in Japan and Industrias Kaiser in Argentina. Datsun/Nissan in Japan also cloned a copy of the Station Wagon and the MB.

At the end of 1952 the CJ-3B was introduced as an interim 1953 model. It featured a higher cowl and grille which were designed to allow for the taller F-headed 'Hurricane' engine. It was a strange looking model which featured a shorter 80-inch wheelbase and a 1,200 lb cargo load.

In 1953, Henry J Kaiser acquired Willys for the princely sum of approximately $60 million. Kaiser was particularly interested in the production facilities at Willys-Overland so that he could increase production of his Kaiser line of automobiles. The company was re-named Willys Motors Inc and then, surprisingly, was left alone to pursue the Jeep product line. The CJ-5 was introduced in 1954. It was still based on the original Jeep specifications but featured the new 'Super Hurricane' L-headed engine, new axles, transmission, seats and a larger, more rounded, body.

The CJ-5 design was crafted off the M38A1 design which Willys had started building for the Army in 1951. The options list offered became

The Army approached Willys with the idea of creating a new generation of Jeep in 1949. Two models were built: the M38 and the M38A1 Initially known as the MC at Willys, it translated into its new Army designation as the M38 which was built in 1950 and 1951. Later it became the civilian CJ-5 in 1954. This 1952 M38A is set up as transportation for a four-star general in Korea. It features headlight guards, blackout light, radio and locking hubs. Owner: David Ciocher.

increasingly long. The basic design of the CJ-5 and the M38A1 remained unaltered until the early sixties when the military took up the M151.

The CJ-5 quickly spawned the CJ-6, featuring a stretched chassis which pulled the 81-inch wheelbase of the CJ-5 up to 101 inches. The body was simply extended with a set of panels designed to fit at an existing body seam. A mass of optional and special equipment was also devised for the new model. Hardtops, two- or four-wheel-drive, seating combinations, three-point hydraulic lifts, dozer blades, post hole diggers, three different power take-offs, pumps, trenchers, air compressors, sprayers and snow ploughs were all part of the offering.

The Jeep 'Dispatcher' DJ-3A was also introduced in the early fifties. This economical two-wheel-drive model was built on the CJ-3B chassis and evolved into one of Jeep's most productive models over the next 40 years with the United States Post Office purchasing thousands of them as mail delivery vehicles.

Above

The M38 series used this L-headed four-cylinder initially rated at 60 hp. Output later increased to 63, 70 and then 72 hp. The production list totals 60,345 M38's built during its production life.

Left

Jeep didn't change the M38A1 too much to create the CJ-5. It remained the tough and rugged working vehicle Jeep had designed for the military. This 1954 CJ-5 is still used as a regular workhorse on a Sonoma County, California, ranch by its owners. Apart from a refreshed four-cylinder engine after 20 years service, the CJ-5 continues to provide reliable service on this mountainous property. Owner: David Best.

Introducing:
America's Lowest Priced
DELIVERY VEHICLE

MODEL DJ 3A HARDTOP

THE 2-WHEEL DRIVE `Jeep` *Dispatcher* →

MODEL DJ 3A CONVERTIBLE TOP

WILLYS . . . MAKERS OF THE WORLD'S MOST USEFUL VEHICLES

Above

Military production raced ahead but Willys were also creating a domestic niche for themselves with an ever increasing variety of models. Interestingly, the most forgotten of Jeep models may be the D-series which has lived the longest production life. Starting out in late 1955, they continued in production until about 1988 at AM General as the Mail Dispatcher for the US Post Office. This Jeep Dispatcher DJ-3A sales literature offers four versions, all of them two-wheel-drive, powered by the Go-Devil four-cylinder engine.

Left

The military and Jeep enjoyed an on-going relationship into the fifties. They looked for ways to improve the product. Jeep eventually created the M170, a field ambulance which could transport the wounded inside the vehicle. It used new front sheet metal, with a higher peak in the hood to provide space for the F-headed engines. Built from the newly designed long wheelbase CJ-6, this 1954 model features a space for two stretchers and medical personnel plus the driver. Owner: Ed Fullerton.

Above

In an effort to liven up their image Willys created this candy-striped Dispatcher named the Surrey. This two-wheel-drive model was designed as the domestic version of the export Gala they had been selling in Mexico, the Caribbean and Central America. Not only did it feature a bright candy pink or blue striped top with fringe around the edge, it had chrome hubcaps, white-walled tyres, a white grille, chrome bumpers and straps like a buggy top running down to the front fenders.

Left

The CJ-5 was introduced in 1955 as a new domestic production model. It was essentially a demilitarized version of the M38A1 and continued in production with only a few changes, including engine options, until 1983. It is shown here in the Willys Jeep promotional photo with its optional tow hitch, hardtop and steel doors.

In 1957 another line was introduced. The Forward Control, or FC, series started out with the FC-150 and quickly evolved into the FC-170. These featured a hoodless cab mounted over the engine like a miniature 18-wheeler. The smaller FC-150 was first built on the 81-inch CJ-5 chassis powered by the F-4 four-cylinder 'Hurricane' engine while the FC-170 was built on the 104-inch wagon-style chassis using the L-6 226 cubic inch 'Super Hurricane' six-cylinder engine.

The Dispatcher line was expanded to include the Surrey, a soft-top, which later evolved into the well known striped top Gala Dispatcher. It sold quite well in the Caribbean and Mexican markets as a rental or for hotel guest transportation. A domestic version of this was also released called 'The Surrey with the Fringe on Top.' It featured a fringed striped top with matching seats in pink, green or blue candy stripes.

The Sixties

A second Jeep revolution happened in the sixties. It was a time of growth in the United States; businesses and private individuals needed specialized automobiles and trucks. The Kaiser automobile line had disappeared and Kaiser were concentrating on developing new products for its profitable Jeep division.

The Army had stopped ordering masses of the M38A1 Jeeps by the late fifties and they had been replaced by the Ford-designed M151 reconnaissance vehicle. In an interesting twist of fate, Jeep now found themselves building Fords alongside Ford, because in 1962 Willys won a competitive bid to build the M151, assembling thousands of them for the US military.

In October, 1962, the new J-Series of pickups and station wagons arrived, based loosely on what Willys had designed in 1946 when they introduced the industry's first all-steel station wagon and pickup. It was called a 'Wagoneer' while the new pickups, based on the same chassis and front sheet metal, were tagged 'Gladiator'.

Powered by the first modern overhead-cam six-cylinder truck engine known as the 'Tornado-OHC' six, they could also be optioned with an automatic transmission which was an 'industry first' for a truck of this size. The Gladiator was offered in pickup and panel truck configurations on either a 120-inch wheelbase for the J-200, or on a 126-inch wheelbase for the J-300 series.

The J-Series and the Wagoneer were offered in two- and four-wheel-drive versions. With these, Kaiser Jeep created the beginnings of what is now termed a 'Sports Utility Vehicle' – one of the most important growth areas for the auto industry in the past 15 years.

These were the first fresh designs from the company since the Station Wagon and Jeepster which didn't have the military in mind. The Wagoneer and Gladiator not only found a huge market with construction, forestry, agricultural and military buyers but evolved a niche with everyday retail buyers who wanted a good looking, purpose-built, all-terrain vehicle for fishing, skiing, off-roading, hunting and hauling boats and trailers.

Right

The M151 'Mutt' ultimately replaced the M38A1 Jeep as the military's light reconnaissance vehicle in 1960. Designed and built by Ford, it was also manufactured by Willys under an Army contract. The new M151's featured fully independent suspensions and are seen here rolling down the Willys production line in 1962. Many of these M151's were used in Vietnam and continue to be used by the US military and other countries.

Below right

New for 1963 was the line of Gladiator trucks and Wagoneer station wagons. Kaiser had just taken over Willys and were able to establish this new line up without a hitch. The new Gladiator pickup was offered in an amazing 47-model range based on half to one ton, two- or four-wheel-drive, cab and chassis, Thriftside or Townside or as a Platform Stake truck. This base model 1963 Gladiator Townside is seen 'feeding the cows' in Santa Barbara County, California.

Above

The 'Tuxedo Park' CJ-5/CJ-6A was a special edition named after a famous country club and introduced in 1964. (From that original Bantam scout car to a country club!) It was specially optioned and aimed at the weekend ski set. During its three-year production run, only 1,000 of these special CJ's were built. This 1966 version is one of 356 assembled that year. When the current owner purchased it, this Tuxedo Park had 36,000 miles on the clock as it had only been used for deer hunting by the first owners. As you can see, it is now a combination of rock crawler and show Jeep. Rebuilt by its new owner, it is now painted in Hot Pink Pearl and features a revised boxed frame, Dana 30 axles, 4 wheel disc brakes, new suspension with lift springs, reversed shackles and axles. It rolls on 15-inch Progressive wheels and Goodrich Mud T/A tyres. The Tuxedo Park is powered by a modified Chevrolet 350 V8 and Turbo 350 automatic transmission. The interior is fully reworked with VDO gauges, custom seats, full roll cage, swing pedals and a custom stereo sound system.
Owner: Tony Lavaqnino.

Above right

Now in its second generation, the Wagoneer station wagon has lost much of its utility appearance allowing Kaiser Jeep to evolve a more luxurious feel with the 1966 Super Wagoneer Station Wagon. It featured three-tone body striping, vinyl roof, chrome roof rack, full wheel hubcaps and white-walled tyres. The Super Wagoneer came with four-wheel-drive and power was supplied from a 327 cubic inch V8.

Right

The Jeepster Commando was a re-invention of the Jeepster, truck and station wagon ideas which Willys had sold so successfully in the early post-war years based on production components and fresh body. Now the Jeepster had the Ford Bronco and the International Scout as sales competitors. Once again the company went to the parts bin and with some creative design work used a mass of production items and a simple sporty looking new body to create a new line of vehicles. The result was the Jeepster Commando pickup, Convertible (1967 as pictured here), or a two-door station wagon.

The mid-sixties marked the beginning of off-road adventuring. The Rubicon Trail in the Sierra Mountains near Lake Tahoe, California, had became one of the ultimate challenges for off-road Jeep enthusiasts. Desert trekking became popular as well as trips down Mexico's Baja peninsula.

In 1963 Willys Jeep changed its name to The Kaiser Jeep Corporation dropping the 'Willys' name from the product line. Apart from the name change, the only production changes came with the addition of the 327 cubic-inch/250 hp 'Vigilante' V8 option which was added in 1965 to the Wagoneer and Gladiator line to improve the overall performance of the J-Series.

By the end of 1965 all the four-wheel drive Universal models were offered with a power take-off option which was designed to run farm and construction equipment. It included a post hole digger, a rotary mower, an implement lift, a winch, a wrecker and a snow plough.

The J-Series was renamed J-2000, J3000 and J-4000 and comprised eight models. A new dual-range transfer case with a simplified shift mechanism was also introduced. The Vigilante was replaced late in the

The Jeepster Commando changed its looks somewhat during its seven year production life. The biggest changes were a V8 power option and new front sheet metal which lost the original Jeep-look with a new abrupt, flat-nosed front end. This change was simple as it only involved the hood and fenders. This 1972 Jeepster Convertible is used for beach transportation in Hawaii.

This beautifully restored 1968 CJ-5 features the 225 cubic inch 'Dauntless' V6. The Jeep is fully restored with a soft top, roll bar, white steel wheels, optional winch and a matching 1945 Bantam civilian trailer with a fold-down tail gate. Owner: David Voll.

sixties with the 350 cubic-inch Dauntless V8 in both models. They also added in 1966 the Dauntless V6 engine to the CJ-5 and CJ-6 as an option. This 155 hp ex-Buick V6 engine more than doubled the base four-cylinder Hurricane engine's 75 hp output.

A military version of the J-Series was also being built called the Universal M-715 Military (ATC). This special version of the J-3000 series came with extra duty suspension, brakes, cooling, a fold-down windshield and a special stake-sided pickup bed.

Within months of the introduction of the revised J-Series, Jeep introduced the first small four-wheel-drive available with automatic transmission, the Jeepster Commando in 1966.

Built on a CJ-6 chassis it was powered by the F-headed Hurricane four-cylinder but could be optioned up with the Dauntless V6 for improved performance. (The Dauntless V6 was actually discontinued by Buick in 1967 and taken up by Jeep.) The Commando was offered in a wide variety of models including a roadster, pickup, convertible pickup and a station wagon. Also introduced in 1966 was the luxury version of the Wagoneer, the Super Wagoneer.

Above left

Under the hood of the 1968 CJ-5 is a 'Dauntless' V6. Jeep sourced the rights and production tooling from Buick who phased the V6 engine out in 1967. It was introduced as an option in late 1966. Owner: David Voll.

Left

The interior of David Voll's 1968 CJ-5 shows how bare and basic the CJ was, right up to the seventies. Only the most necessary gauges and controls were fitted.

Above

In 1968 George Barris, Hollywood's famous 'Kustom' car builder, created this four-door, four-seater CJ-5 for Ross Bagasarian, the creator of the TV series The Chipmunks. *The Barris shop stretched the frame and fabricated a new body by splicing together a pair of CJ-5 bodies. A new safari top was stitched up and airliner seats were installed front and rear for more comfort. George also added chrome wheels with Firestone high performance 'red-wall' street tyres. For more pep, a small block Chevrolet V8 was installed. The job was so well done it looked like a factory built unit. (George Barris)*

The Seventies

In the seventies four-wheel-drive vehicles made a major leap from utility to luxury family motoring. The beginning of the decade brought a change of ownership when the American Motors Corporation purchased the Kaiser Jeep for $10 million in February 1970.

Significant changes in production and company management were made when American Motors Corporation (AMC) split the company into two units, AMC and AM General. AMC was to build civilian Jeeps in Toledo, Ohio, and AM General took over military vehicle production in an old Studebaker plant in South Bend, Indiana.

The booming four-wheel-drive market was buoyed by Jeep winning the Baja 1000 off-road race and many of the events organized by the newly formed SCORE organization which was running races in the California and Nevada deserts.

The Jeep line-up in the mid-seventies included an improved Gladiator now called the J-10 and J-20, the re-styled Commando, the Cherokee Chief (a two-door Wagoneer), Wagoneer and Custom Wagoneer, the Commando, and the CJ-5 and CJ-7 models. The CJ-5 went through another evolution when the Renegade was introduced, powered by a 304 cubic-inch AMC V8.

From the Renegade V8 came the 'Super Jeep'. It was painted in bright colours with contrasting racing stripes, custom interior trim, special wheels, fender extensions and roll bar. It was the first serious sporty CJ.

In 1973 the Commando model was dropped while the Wagoneer went through several convolutions with the introduction of Quadra-Trac, and an automatic full-time 4WD system. The following year the Jeep Renegade was back as a production model based on the CJ-5.

AM General also achieved great success building a revised Dispatcher for the US Postal Service as mail delivery vehicles. Many of them are still being used across the country for daily deliveries.

AMC worked for four years to replace the CJ-5. Finally, in 1976, the seventh generation of civilian Jeep appeared, as the CJ-7. Built on a longer 93.5-inch wheelbase, it was produced alongside the CJ-5.

In an effort to enliven the CJ-5's image, AMC did a short run of Super Jeeps. These Super Jeeps were bedecked with a wild stripe package, bigger wheels and tyres, chrome bumpers, special interior trim and a V8 option.

Jeep were ready for the seventies but their parent company, Kaiser Industries, were not. They sold off Jeep in February of 1970 to American Motors who took the company on with gusto and a bright vision of a four-wheel-drive future. The basic CJ-5 continued in production, unaltered. This stock AMC Jeep shows the most basic 1974 CJ-5 Universal on a construction sight as the boss's wagon.

Renault, the French automobile manufacturer, wanted a foothold into the American market so it purchased nearly half of AMC in 1979. It was to prove a strange combination of cultures and talents with AMC eventually selling Renault passenger cars, Renault funding the development of the new Cherokee and transferring some of its best design staff to AMC.

By the end of the decade sports utility vehicles had seized a huge sector of the new car market. Jeep were not alone. Ford, International, Chevy and Chrysler all had new offerings in this developing market; and Land Rover in the UK were more than happy with the new trend.

Above

The base model of the Wagoneer line was the Cherokee Chief two-door station wagon. This 1975 version features some of AMC's first bold graphics which later became common on off-road vehicles. The Wagoneer line used a torsion bar front suspension and could be ordered with a stock 258 cubic inch six-cylinder, 360 or 401 V8. It could also be had with several drive options, including the automatic Quadra-Trac which is fitted to this version.

Left

This 1975 Jeep Pioneer J-20 Townside heavy duty pickup is decked out in its deluxe packaging with bucket seats, chrome truck mirrors and a woody side-paneling. The J-20 was the 3/4-ton version based on the old Gladiator series pickups and featured a 130-inch wheelbase and a 360 cubic-inch V8 as standard. AMC/Jeep focused on selling the J-20 as a 'working man's pickup'.

Above

American Motors used Jeep as a flagship division. They poured a heaping of advertising and development dollars into the division and came up with some creative packaging. This included the 1976 CJ-7 Renegade 'Levi' model which featured the interior trimmed in the same cotton material as Levi Jeans. This Renegade package also featured a roll bar, alloy wheels, a graphic stripes package and new 'double window' doors. The CJ-7 also made Jeep history as the first CJ to offer automatic transmission and the Quadra-Trac drive system. Six-cylinder or V8 engines were offered.

Above right

The truck division at AMC/Jeep continued slowly to develop the J-series pickups. This 1976 Townside pickup is a J-10 model on the longer 130.7-inch wheelbase chassis. A shorter 118.7-inch version was standard and a heavy duty J-20 was also offered in both configurations. Two- and four-wheel-drive versions were offered with a 360 cubic inch V8 as the base engine. Optional engines included 360 and 401 ci V8's.

Right

This rear view of the 1976 Renegade CJ-5 Universal shows how tidily the new one-piece rear window convertible top looked and worked. The spare was mounted on the rear instead of the side, improving driving clearance. It also featured the new rubber fender flares which allowed designers to add wider wheels to improve traction, looks and stability.

Above

The CJ-7 was an instant hit. Gone were the wavy hip-line door mouldings and in their place was a conventional passenger car-style door. The CJ-7 offered more leg room front and rear along with improved safety and handling. This 1977 Renegade package came with pressed off-road wheels and Goodyear tyres, rubber wheel arch flares, a hardtop, a roll bar and graphics.

Left

The popularity of mega-Jeeps has become a national movement in the nineties. This white 1978 CJ-7 has been extensively reworked and hot-rodded with a 400 hp 350 Chevy V8 and Turbo 400 automatic transmission. The suspension and wheels have also been completely revised with over-axle spring mounts, a 3-inch body lift, 2-1/2-inch raised shackles and 4-inch raised Trailmaster springs. This has effectively raised the height of the CJ about 15 inches. Added to this are 44-inch Dick Cepek off-road tyres which give the Jeep a mini-monster truck look. Owner: Anthony Portillo.

Above

This gold bronze CJ-5 from 1979 features the more dramatic Renegade stripe package roll bar and stamped steel wheels, capped with Goodyear Tracker off-road tyres which had become popular by this time. The Golden Eagle CJ-7 was also introduced this year as a deluxe model which included a composite hardtop.

Below right

Looking to give the J-series a sportier look, AMC offered the J-10 Townside pickup in Honcho livery. Available with both straight six and V8 engines and two- and four-wheel-drive, the J-trucks had a long and illustrious working life. This 1979 version features a huge side-panels graphic in three colours over the base colour. The Honcho idea evolved in 1976 and changed every year until 1987 at which time the J-trucks ceased production after the successful introduction of the mid-sized Comanche pickups.

Right

Superlift Suspension Systems, the after-market 4x4 suspension parts company from West Monroe, Louisiana, developed this Jeep as a 'Petersen's 4 Wheel and Off-Road magazine' project vehicle and as a 'rolling laboratory for certifying new products.' Built for good looks and off-road capability, this CJ-7 is finished in brilliant Subaru Electric Yellow and Ford Grabber Blue Jeep and features Superlift Suspension with 4-inch Superlift springs, triple front shocks, dual Air Locker differentials, Superlift steering and body lift. It is powered by a fuel-injected AMC 360 V8 and rolls on 33-inch Hoosier tyres and Boyd wheels. Owner: Superlift Suspension Systems.

The Eighties

A new model based on the CJ-7's mechanicals and body panels known as the 'Scrambler' (CJ-8) used a special 103.5-inch chassis to create a stylish 'import fighting' pickup truck. It came with a fibreglass hard top, roll bar and could be upgraded with all the regular CJ-7 options.

But this was not the big news at Jeep. An intensive and in depth market research programme had been ongoing to look at future products, which culminated in a programme to develop a model. This was to become the marque's most successful vehicle venture ever.

Their research had found that future markets lay in compact sports utility vehicles: Renault and AMC pumped $250 million into design and production of the new compact XJ Cherokee and Wagoneer sportswagons. They were introduced to the Press at Borrego Springs, California, in late 1983 and immediately received rave reviews.

It was a revolution and AMC's timing could not have been better. The new Cherokee was unique – it was the only compact sport utility vehicle to offer either a two-door and four-door model and it was built as a unibody rather than using a traditional chassis and frame construction. Neither Ford nor Chevrolet would match this four-door design feature for another six years. Power was supplied by either a four-cylinder base model engine or an upline option 2.8 litre V6. This engine was obtained from Chevrolet but was replaced in 1987 by AMC's own 4.0 litre in-line six. The new Cherokee was an immediate hit and sales took off in both two and four-door versions. It won the coveted '4x4 of the Year' from three major magazines.

Several four-wheel-drive systems, including Command Trac and Selec-Trac, offered either part-time or full-time four-wheel traction. Various interior and exterior styling, comfort and off-road performance packages were also offered. The model line continued largely unchanged into the nineties, although many revisions and improvements were made to the Cherokee line.

The new Cherokee was not the only 4WD revolution to emerge from AMC during the mid-eighties. The ageing CJ-5 was discontinued in 1985 but production of the CJ-7 and Scrambler pickup continued. The

Right

The Scrambler, or CJ-8, was another derivation of the CJ-7. Introduced in 1981 it was mechanically identical to the CJ-7 and continued in production until the early eighties. The Scrambler featured a hardtop cab, roll bar and a pickup bed trimmed with an optional wood stake panel. This rare 1983 model is still in daily use and is loved by its owner for its good looks and reliability. Owner: Mary Jane Lendall.

Below right

The XJ-series Cherokee and Wagoneer Ltd were introduced in 1984 (1988 model shown). It was the first product from AMC after Renault purchased nearly half the company in 1979. Available in either two- or four-doors it was powered by a 2.5 litre four-cylinder, or an optional 2.8 litre Chevy V6. Its unique Unibody construction eliminated the traditional 4x4 chassis. It used coil springs up front with leaf springs on the rear. This body is still in production, virtually unaltered, ten years later.

CJ-7 was finally abandoned and replaced with the Jeep Wrangler (YJ) in the spring of 1986 as an 1987 model. The first production model rolled off the production line on 12 March 1986 at AMC's Brampton, Canada, assembly plant.

The Wrangler sourced much of its hardware from the Cherokee line including wider axles, larger brakes and improved steering. Its styling was based on the traditional and rugged Universal CJ series but the Wrangler also offered improved ride and comfort. AMC also spun off another pickup model from the new XJ Cherokee model. Known as the Comanche pickup it used much of the body, suspension, and power train from the XJ and was sold in four- and six-cylinder models and two- and four-wheel-drive.

Competing with Detroit's Big Three had taken its toll on AMC and its resources. Even with the success of the new Cherokee and Wrangler lines, AMC were doing poorly in the automobile market with their only other products being the Eagle sedan and wagon, carry-over models from the ancient 1970 Hornet and a couple of Renault-built sedans.

AMC lacked the finance to fund the development of a new automobile line up but they managed to survive with Jeep as their only supporting division.

But the future was once again dramatically reshaped when, on 5 August 1987, Lee Iacocca purchased the American Motors Corporation on behalf of the Chrysler Corporation.

It was a wise move. Chrysler needed a recreational vehicle line and had neither the money nor time to develop one. This purchase gave them the crown jewel of the marketplace – Jeep. With this purchase came not only Jeep's great new product line-up but a dealer network, assembly plants and parts division. The AMC/Renault car line was discarded within 18 months but the Jeep line was left intact. Chrysler formed a new division under its Dodge, Plymouth, Chrysler dealer network called Jeep/Eagle. This new division was to market the Jeep and a new upmarket line-up of Eagle automobiles.

Right

The 1986 Comanche pickup was a spin-off of the XJ-series wagons. The pickup truck arrived with a seven foot bed which made it a 'mid-sized' pickup. In 1987 the engines were refreshed and the Chevy V6 was replaced with the AMC in-line six. Available in both two- and four-wheel-drive the Comanche then found a niche in the market, just as the earlier Gladiator had, as a tough work horse. A variety of sport packages were also offered for the Comanche with alloy wheels, light-bars, body graphics and special interiors.

Below right

The popularity of modifying CJ's is perfectly displayed in this stunning metallic Marina Blue CJ-7. Built by its owner this CJ-7 now runs a 350 hp 350 Chevy V8. The engine features a Tunnel Ram manifold topped with two 450 cfm Holley carburettors and polished Street Scoop. The Jeep features a total body lift of 28 inches including 15 x 10-inch Alcoa alloy wheels capped with 44-inch Dick Cepek tyres. The interior is all custom, with a polished stainless steel dash, Auto Meter instruments, a super sound system and a custom roll cage which incorporates a short convertible top. Owner: Steve Fasano.

The Nineties

With the incredible growth of the recreational vehicle market in the eighties, Jeep has continued to flower into the nineties. On 22 March 1990, Jeep turned out their one millionth automobile (civilian Jeep), a red XJ Cherokee Limited at their Toledo, Ohio, assembly plant.

Jeep has become an exporter and international builder. Jeeps are now assembled at a plant in China and Cherokees are built under a licensing agreement with Beijing Jeep. The parent company have also developed a relationship with Steyr-Daimler-Punch in Graz, Austria, assembling Grand Cherokees for the European marketplace.

In another decisive move, Jeep also developed a right-hand-drive version of the Cherokee. This had a two-fold effect. It produced a model suitable for rural mail carriers who needed a right-hand-drive vehicle to safely deliver the mail and, of more major consequence, provided the engineering work to design a suitable export model for Britain, Australia and Japan, who require or prefer right-hand-drive models.

In 1991 the Wrangler line up was revised slightly with the introduction of the Jeep Renegade which was repackaged with 'Power-Tech Six',

The Wrangler appeared in 1987 replacing the CJ-7 which itself had replaced the CJ-5 earlier in the decade. The new Wrangler was better engineered, offered a wider track, improved ride and braking and more comfort. It shared more mechanically with the Jeep Cherokee than it did with the CJ-7. In the next ten years, it changed little in the way of engineering but would feature a wild assortment of paint and model packages. This 1990 'Islander' package was aimed at the Hawaiian and Caribbean rent-a-Jeep customers.

Build a new model and someone will always try to outdo you. RSW from St Augustin-Buisdorf, Germany, turned on all the tricks to build the ultimate Wrangler. It is known as the 'Giant'. Finished in Black with a Hot Yellow convertible top, the Wrangler stands 87 inches high and 88 inches wide. It features giant fender flares and running boards, custom 4-inch chrome tube bumpers, a light bar, air horns and a mass of stainless steel fittings. Power is supplied via a 350 Chevy V8 running four Weber carburettors and automatic transmission. The body is lifted 4 inches with an RSW Lift Kit, Rancho RS9000 shock absorbers, ConFerr spring shackles and a 7-inch RSW body Lift Kit. Builder: RSW St Augustin-Buisdorf, Germany.

a 180 hp version of the 4.0 litre in-line six-cylinder engine from the Cherokee. Other packages have been introduced including the brightly coloured Islander and military-look Sahara with its low-gloss Sage and Army Green-painted body work.

The basic model line-up of Jeeps has not changed much in the first half of the nineties except for the addition of one new model, the Grand Cherokee, in 1992. But within each sector of the model line-up Jeep has produced some amazing growth.

In 1992 the XJ-series Cherokee offered 42 different basic models with 56 options or option packages, adding up to over 2,352 variations. The Wrangler has only two base models with two engines and 32 option or option packages, making up a base of 128 different Wrangler packages. The Commanche pickup was finally dropped from production in 1992, as Chrysler felt it competed directly with its own, mid-sized Dodge Dakota pickup.

The ZJ-series Grand Cherokee burst onto the market place as the ultimate luxury off-road recreational touring wagon in the spring of 1992 as a 1993 model. Initially it was powered by a 190 hp version of Jeep's 'Power-Tech' in-line six-cylinder engine. The Grand Cherokee was an instant success, taking sales away from every other off-road vehicle builder including Ford, Toyota, Nissan, Range Rover and Chevrolet.

Like the British Range Rover, the Grand Cherokee offered style, performance, luxury and comfort but the Grand Cherokee came into the market at a far more reasonable price. A further blow to Land Rover on its home turf was the introduction in 1995 in the UK of the Cherokee 2.5 Turbo Diesel, the 4x4 market over there being dominated by diesels. The engine is actually one of the Turbotronic family which

has been developed by VM Motori SpA in Cento, Italy – 116bhp at 4,000rpm, 207 lb ft at 2,000rpm – the Turbotronic diesel already powers Chrysler's Voyager, the world's best selling MPV.

Jeep had one more model to add to this winning new range: the Grand Wagoneer Limited. The Grand Wagoneer Limited was introduced as the ultimate luxury performance model powered by an electronically fuel-injected 5.2 litre V8 engine sourced from Chrysler's parts bin. (This engine is now available in any Grand Cherokee model.)

In 1995 the new Grand Cherokee is offered in an Orvis Edition, melding Jeep's off-road capabilities with one of North America's premier fly fishing and hunting equipment manufacturers.

Above

In 1990 Jeep introduced the Wrangler 'Sahara'. It was based on the regular Wrangler model and was available in a flat drab-olive metallic. This gave the Sahara a military look. It came with mesh-guarded fog lights, a special interior package, special Sahara decals, steel wheels and fender flares.

Left

Known as 'the Mini Giant' this wild Wrangler has been extensively reworked by RSW in St Augustin-Buisdorf, Germany. It now features a 5.7 litre Chevy V8 which has been tricked up with a slew of performance accessories and chrome. The body uses an RSW flare kit to cover the 15x12-inch Alcoa alloy wheels, a 3-inch body lift, along with ConFerr springs and lift shackles. The body also features stainless steel bumpers and roll cage, light guard and grille cover. Inside, Mini Giant has been revised with Scheel-Mann 'Traveller' seats, VDO instruments, leather trim, centre console and a Raid leather-bound steering wheel. Owner: RSW St Augustin-Buisdorf, Germany.

Above

The new Jeep Cherokee introduced in 1984 was a result of
Jeep realising that the future of recreational vehicles lay in
compact vehicles, not full-sized models. Ten years later it continues in production with a wide assortment of models being
offered. This 1990 Cherokee Laredo features four doors, flared
wheel arches, fog lamps and alloy wheels.

Above right

Jeep re-invented the Jeep with a clever new body package
called the Renegade in 1991. It looked like a Wrangler on
steroids and was aimed at folks who loved the Jeep look but
didn't really want to go off-road. The body was reworked with
a flared fender kit, new bumpers, diamond plate axle and
sump guard. It is finished in red with a matching red interior.
It was powered by the new 180 hp, in-line 'Power-Tech Six'
cylinder engine.

Right

The Grand Wagoneer was still selling in 1991. The new
Grand Wagoneer had not yet been introduced but it was the
swan song for a great model which had started in 1963 as the
Wagoneer and had evolved into a second line known as the
Cherokee. By the time the model was finished, it had become
a V8-powered luxury Sport wagon with refined looks, interior,
power and handling to match.

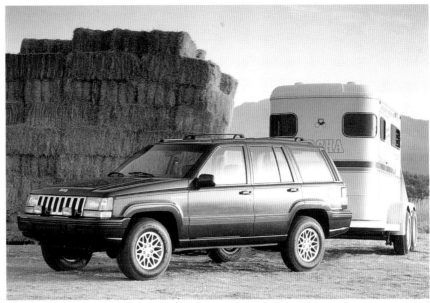

Above

In 1992, Jeep introduced its first completely new vehicle in ten years, the Grand Cherokee. Sold as a 1993 model, sales accelerated at such a startling pace that Jeep have had a hard time keeping their dealers supplied with vehicles. It won instant praise from the Press including the '1993 Truck of the Year Award' from Motor Trend Magazine. Offered with both six and V8 power, the new model provided some terrific on-road handling and high speed touring, while retaining Jeep's heritage as a 'mountain goat' off-road. Many people have also found it perfect for hauling horses and boat trailers. The 1993 Grand Wagoneer version is seen here.

Left

The Wrangler continues to be a popular model, not only with buyers but as a vacation rent-a-car. On the Hawaiian islands you can rent Wranglers for touring and exploring. A day at the beach, an off-road trek across an ancient rocky lava flow – the Jeep is the perfect Hawaiian explorer.

Above

The aftermarket has now started to work on the Jeep Grand
Cherokee. This RSW/Desert Ox conversion from Germany
was built to suit the needs of high-speed continental touring. It
features a new 'Front Effect' nose with built-in driving lights,
Desert Ox running boards and light guards. RSW fender flares
added to the effect which extends the body line over the
8.5x17-inch AZEV forged-alloy wheels capped with 255/50 R
General XP tyres. The suspension has been reworked with an
RSW lowering kit, stabilizer bar and Bilstein gas shock
absorbers. The interior is also custom, with leather Scheel-
Mann seats, Burlwood trim and a wood/leather trimmed air
bag steering wheel. Builder: RSW St Augustin-Buisdorf,
Germany.

Above right

George Barris of Barris Kustom Industries in North Hollywood,
California, created this custom 1994 Grand Cherokee for his
wife Shirley. George had Dick Dean rework the body with a
new fibreglass nose, running boards and a Continental spare
moulded into the rear door. It was then repainted in House of
Kolors White/Gold Pearl and Gold Pearl featuring a broad centre stripe. The V8-powered Grand Cherokee now rolls on SEC
alloy wheels with custom finished Goodrich tires featuring gold
bands. (George Barris)

Right

Since its introduction, the Wrangler has gone through only a
few trim and technical changes. This 1994 Wrangler was used
in an episode on the history of Jeep for the TV show
Automobiles on the A & E – History Channel. It was also
used for a series of fishing adventures into the Sierra Nevada
mountains in search of wild trout.

Above

The 1995 Grand Cherokee has been packaged into a special Orvis Edition. Orvis have been specializing in high-quality fly-fishing equipment since 1856 and wanted to create a limited-edition Jeep Grand Cherokee. Available in only one colour, Moss Green Pearl Coat, it features distinctive leather-trimmed seats in Champagne and Dark Green with red piping. Underneath it has full-time Quadra-Trac 4x4, 'Up-Country' suspension and Trailer Tow package. Power is delivered from a stock 4.0 litre in-line six.

Left

The 1995 Wrangler model continues to use location name tags. This 'Rio Grande' is finished in Bright Mango with light tan top.

Above

There is still a high degree of hand assembly work on the Wrangler production line in Toledo. All of the upper structure, electrical, glass and most of the interior is installed before the body is mated to the chassis on the production line. It's a two-person team, assembling left and right. Here the complete dashboard assembly is fitted ready to hook up to the wiring loom further down the line.

Left

Here, raw Wrangler body units are electrically welded together by two-man teams working on specific assembly points left and right. Once the body is fully assembled, it heads into the paint booth.

The Future –
plus some R&R

If any division of Detroit's Big Three manufacturers has a bright future, then Jeep/Eagle must be the star at the top of the tree. Its product line is diverse and growing, its designers are young and talented and its engineering staff are proven experts on the capabilities of on- and off-road automobiles.

Jeep Design is currently headed by Trevor M Creed who has been responsible for Jeep products during the past five years. Creed has watched the market grow immensely for light recreational vehicles such as Jeeps in the last ten years and notes with pleasure that 'it's the biggest growth there has been in the past five years, with Jeep having expanded every model line to suit this increasing demand for these rugged and luxurious vehicles.'

Now headquartered in Auburn Hills, Michigan, at Chrysler's new world headquarters, the Jeep design team have access to all of Chrysler's test facilities and tracks. On-road and off-road testing can take place in private during the heat of summer and in the frigid depths of a northern winter. Testing of new suspensions and powertrains also takes place over such courses as the Rubicon Trail in California, the Mojave Desert in summer and during off-road racing.

True to their word to make Jeep the premier off-road builder in the world, Chrysler have funded a series of Jeep concept cars during the past few years. These have included a proposed mini-Jeep (code-named the JJ) which did not see light of day. It was originally designed to compete with the Suzuki Sidekick, but other concepts, including the J2000 and the Concept 1 – which are both full-sized futuristic four-door wagons – and the miniature Ecco, have all been exhibited extensively on the show circuit.

The future of Jeep is bright. With assembly plants in the United States now working at full capacity and the combination of a healthy export market of either assembled models or models built at plants in China and Austria, Jeep is surfing the wave of success.

Trevor M Creed is the Director of Advanced, Exterior/ Jeep/Truck and Interior Design, Colour & Trim at Jeep. This means Creed designs and directs the interior and exterior styling of all Jeep products. It's an exciting job which combines design studio work with field engineering and testing. His team of designers creates everything for the Jeep except the mechanical, chassis and powertrain pieces.

The Jeep 'Concept 1' show car was originally displayed at the 1989 Detroit Auto Show. Created initially as a design exercise, it became the precursor to the all-new ZJ Grand Cherokee introduced in 1993.

The new Wrangler replacement model is due in 1996 and others will follow within the next few years as the Cherokee is replaced and the model line-up expanded. By the year 2000 all current Jeep models will be replaced, putting Jeep in a great position to tread lightly into the next century.

Jeeps at Work

The Jeep was designed to be a mechanical mule, ready for action and capable of taking an immense pounding and still keep going. As history has so positively shown, the world owes much to the Jeep and its designers at Bantam, Willys and Ford, who pulled together a vehicle which affected the outcome of the Second World War.

The military continued its love affair with the Jeep long after the last cannon fire was heard in 1945 and the returning soldiers knew about the mighty Jeep's versatility. The following pictures (pages 95-103) give some indication of the range of application whch was born out of that foreknowledge of the Jeep's capabilities. Jeeps were put to work in virtually every facet of public and business life.

They continued to serve in the public interest as fire and emergency trucks, postal delivery wagons, rental vehicles, police and security vehicles and snow ploughs, as tour buses, farm vehicles to pull ploughs, mount compressors and pull trailers, as tugs for aircraft and rail cars and as tow wagons for boats at steep launching ramps. Jeeps have also been put to work as recreational vehicles taking fishermen, hunters and campers into the back country to pursue their hobbies and sports.

Jeep Jamborees

Back in the early fifties a Jeep enthusiast named Mark Smith formed the Jeepers Jamboree and expanded it to a nationwide organization which worked with Jeep to promote environmentally friendly off-road adventures. (See pictures on pages 104 to 110.)

Smith and his group have worked hard to promote the proper use of public lands and over the past 40 years have taken more than 25,000 vehicles and 70,000 people over the famous Rubicon trail in California. At events like these, folks discovered that the Jeep is an exceptional recreational vehicle.

The Ecco was developed to promote 4x4 and the smart use of 4x4's outdoors. It is aimed at being an environmentally friendly back-country vehicle for the next century. It is designed as a lightweight, two-door, four-passenger go-anywhere vehicle powered by a fuel-efficient 1.5 litre three-cylinder, two-stroke engine producing 85 hp. The body is made of 100% recyclable materials and features a four-wheel-drive system with plenty of ground clearance using fully independent suspension. It is concepts like the Ecco which show how bright the future can be for good design and smart engineering.

This is the original CJ-5 tour Jeep modified by San Juan Scenic Jeep Tours back in 1959. It was set up with seats for three plus the driver, with a lunch and coffee box mounted off the tailgate. It took thousands of tourists to such interesting man-made and natural wonders as Mystery Mountain Gold Mine and Imogene Pass. Owner: San Juan Scenic Jeep Tours, Ouray, Colorado.

This education has opened up Jeep owners' understanding of both their vehicle and the ethics of exploring the back country in their Jeeps. Weekend trips into the Rockies, the California Desert and the Appalachian mountains by Jeep clubs have flowered along with the Jeep Jamboree USA organization.

The Jamborees are now run around the nation with the support of Chrysler's Jeep/Eagle division so devotees can learn about and enjoy their Jeeps off-road.

The Jamboree schedule is run for ten months of the year and features the Rubicon Trail in California, the deserts of Utah, the forests of New England and Maine, the swamps of the Everglades, and a trip across the top of the Rocky mountains between Telluride and Ouray, Colorado.

Each Jamboree event is trail-rated and designed to take Jeep tours safely into America's backwoods on back country trails which have been evaluated by a Trail Boss who leads the Jamboree. It's a great way to discover the ruggedness and versatility of the Jeep and its proper use in difficult off-road situations.

Above left

San Juan Scenic Jeep Tours Jeep rental business has been in existence since 1946, when the company was started by Buddy Davis as Colorado's first Jeep tour company. This 1958 CJ-5 was part of the fleet of Jeeps rented out by Francis Kuboske who purchased the company in 1959. It gave sterling service to tourists, fishermen and back country explorers who wanted to see the top of the Colorado Rockies. Owner, above and left: San Juan Scenic Jeep Tours, Ouray, Colorado.

Left

It's easy to see why these Willys Station Wagons, built by San Juan Scenic Jeep Tours, made such great tour wagons. The roof and side windows could be trimmed to the sills leaving the front doors functioning perfectly and the high-placed seats gave everyone a great view. This 1953 8-passenger wagon was converted with heavy-duty suspension and uprated with a six-cylinder Willys engine. It is seen here on a log bridge which crossed one of the many mountains creeks on the way to the Tom Boy Mine in the Silver San Juan mountains above Ouray..

Above

This was a favourite trick of tour driver Jim Ashley when he took his tour groups for San Juan Scenic Jeep Tours to Oh' Point back in the early sixties. Today Oh' Point is closed off. This 1952 Station Wagon was converted to carry eight passengers with the roof cut off to the door sills. It was a four-cylinder wagon with a three-speed transmission and did a sterling job for many years.

Left

Some guys get right into their work! Bill Delaney shot this great photo of Rick Russell inching down this cliff face in his CJ-6. Rick owns Sidekick Off Road Maps, a company specialising in producing off-road maps and videos in Chino, California, so Rick knows what it takes to get into and out of the back country. He built this custom 1956 CJ-6 as the perfect go-anywhere machine. The Jeep now takes him deep into the back country on mapping and filming expeditions and as you can see, he can get hung-up in his work. The Jeep is built from a CJ-6 with custom chassis modifications, is powered by a 350 Chevy V8 and fitted out with a full roll cage, high lift suspension, off-road wheels and drivetrain with Detroit Locker differentials. Rick is seen here inching down a cliff on the way out of a trip to the California ghost town of Panamint City. He is hanging off one the Warn winches fitted to the Jeep for such occasions. Panamint City is 6,000 ft up in the Panamint Mountains of eastern California and is only accessible via this washed out road. Owners: Rick and Marilyn Russell. (Photo: Bill Delaney)

Above left

This 1954 CJ-5 has been a workhorse on a Sonoma County farm for years. It is used for all kinds of chores from towing machinery to toting feed to horses in lower pastures to hauling in firewood and maybe zipping down to the lake for a swim. It is a firm favourite with the children too, who have been lucky enough to learn to drive the CJ around the farm.
Owners: David Best & Maggie Roth.

Above

The FC series or Forward Control Jeeps were not that popular until folks realised how valuable they were as workhorses. With the cab mounted up over the engine, the greater part of the chassis could be used for cargo and hauling. Two versions were built: the FC-150 based on the CJ-5 chassis, and the larger six-cylinder power FC-170 based on the station wagon chassis. Built between 1957 and 1964 they were converted to many uses including fire trucks and utility company work vehicles. They are considered desirable by collectors these days and good ones are hard to find.

Above

A final trip with San Juan Jeep Tours. They custom built this 11-seater J-20 to take tours into the Rocky Mountains around Ouray and Teluride Colorado. Bernie Kuboske and his crew at the tour company built a series of these J-20's powered by factory 360 V8s with four-speed transmissions. Both axles run 4.11 gears and have re-rated suspensions, wheels and tyres. Bernie and his tour guides have completed over 100,000 accident-free miles in this and the other J-20's in their fleet, bridging 13,000-ft mountain passes every day over rough back country roads. This 1977 J-20 is at the old Queen Anne Mine in the Silver San Juan Mountains, outside Silverton, Colorado. Owner: San Juan Scenic Jeep Tours, Ouray, Colorado.

Above right

The fire fighters at the Hopatcong Fire Department in New Jersey have this 1987 Comanche pickup which is used as their multi-purpose firehouse vehicle. In the winter it is fitted out with a snow plow and is used to clear the way for the fire trucks.

Right

Police departments across the US love the Jeep Cherokee. Fitted with 'Command-Trac' part-time four-wheel-drive system, 4.0 litre six-cylinder engine and the five-speed manual transmission, this model is retrofitted with a police light bar, radio equipment and rescue equipment supplies. This 1993 model pictured in Ouray, Colorado, is used for all police duties from traffic control to patrol and search and rescue.

Above

The Hopatcong Police Department have this new Cherokee which is used lightly during the summer and then 24 hours-a-day during winter in mid-state New Jersey. The town of Hopatcong is situated on beautiful Lake Hopatcong and every kind of summer and winter emergency can be called to this station. Having the flexibility of a full four-wheel-drive Cherokee makes good sense for a police department which has to deal with summer crowds and winter snows.

Left

The Hopatcong Fire Department in New Jersey is a big Jeep fan. They also have this 1986 J-10 Townside, used exclusively as a Cascade Air Truck and based at their Northwood Engine Company No. 2 station. In this configuration it carries air tanks to refill breathing apparatus during a fire emergency. This is done from six refillable air tanks in the bed of the pickup. The J-10 is powered by a factory 360 V8 with an automatic transmission.

Trails are rated on a scale of one to ten. Ten is the most difficult. Many of the Jamborees are rated 2-6 meaning that most stock Jeeps can traverse the trail with care. On trails rated 8-9, the Trail Boss and his helpers assist all drivers through the most difficult sections.

The Jeep Jamboree organization supports the works of the Tread Lightly organization which is working to keep public lands open for public use by educating off-roaders on the ethics of traversing back-country trails, without harming nature or the environment.

Above left

The ultimate tell-tale for all Jeep Jamboree participants is this 'Jeep Jamborees USA' spare tyre cover. It signifies that you have been there and back on a Jamboree and that sensible off-roading is your sport.

Left

Getting a front tyre changed proved a difficult task on this Everglades Jamboree because of the soft ground and the angle at which the Jeep sat on the track. The tyre had been damaged by a Swamp Cypress root which stuck out into the trail like a railway spike. Don Sherman (on the left) saved the day by finding a large curved tree branch which he managed to jam under the front of the Grand Cherokee so the front could be levered up to change the tyre.

Above

The first section of the Ouray Jeep Jamboree in the Colorado Rocky Mountains travels a spectacular one-lane trail which had been hand-cut and blasted out of the rock face 120 years ago by miners seeking gold up in the mountains. The cliff above stretches straight up 300 ft or more, while the cliff below drops straight off the side of the road into a creek several hundred feet below. It is not a trail for those afraid of heights.

Above

The Seminole Jeep Safari in the Everglades Swamp in Florida proved to be an interesting trip especially if you liked mud. This one section through a cypress forest taxed your driving skills but only a few inexperienced drivers got stuck. All were jerked free with Snatch'em Straps and the adventures continued to the next bog hole.

Left

On the last leg of the Ouray Jeep Jamboree there is one final creek crossing to traverse on the way out of the Uncompahgre National Forest. Most drivers make this the big splash at the end of the day, washing off the undersides after the dusty trip over 13,000 ft Engineers Pass.

Above

This modified 1946 CJ-2A, driven by Dave Green on a recent Rubicon adventure, had been well prepared for tough trail work. Dave wanted to retain its vintage feel and look and also wanted a tougher drivetrain. To achieve this he installed a 1952 F-head four-cylinder engine and re-engineered it under-neath with pieces from a 1966 CJ-5. The CJ-2A also features a winch, high profile off-road tyres, lift kit, Rancho shocks, Superlift springs, locking hubs and a rear rack to carry extra fuel and provisions. It is a perfect off-road vintage Jeep which not only looks good but does its job like a battle trooper. Owner: Dave Green.

Right

The Rubicon Trail has become the ultimate Jeep challenge for the past twenty years. This Jamboree is run by Mark Smith, head of the Jeepers Jamboree from Georgetown, California, and follows an old Native American footpath which took the Indian people over the Sierra Nevada mountains to Lake Tahoe. It is rated as 'Ten' because of the rugged terrain and can be traversed only by experienced Jeepers in modified Jeeps such as the ones pictured.

Above

'Hang on!' was the call on this difficult section of the Rubicon Trail. The trail has some tough sections which require driving skill beyond the normal trail riding. This rocky pinch in the very first section of the Rubicon takes expert navigation to clear without damaging the vehicle. This 1960 CJ-5 is driven by Robert Wascher and is powered by a 350 Chevy V8. It is expertly set up with a full roll cage, Warn winch, spare fuel cans, trail rack, lift kit, oversized Dick Cepek tyres and body plating. Camping equipment is carried on top of the roll cage. Owner: Robert Wascher.

Right

Some sections of the Rubicon Trail are easily traversed but the trail needs constant care and attention as it crosses the granite ridges of the Sierra Nevada range. This bright yellow CJ-7 is driven with the help of an observer, who checked on conditions on the right-hand side as the Jeep moved over and down a small granite ridge in the trail.

The Ideal Jeep Wrangler Trail Package

Like any production vehicle, the Jeep is the sum of a designer's efforts to mix production realities with basic everyday use. In its most basic production form the Wrangler can traverse any public highways but given the extremes found off-road, some additions are necessary.

Equipping a Wrangler with a selection of Jeep options and aftermarket parts will afford the owner better traction, improved comfort, a bigger safety margin and better ground clearance which add up to the Wrangler being able to go far into the back country with a greater margin of safety and personal security. Bob Dibble from Bishop, California, created this repackaged Wrangler using a new 1993 Wrangler he purchased from Don-A-Vee Jeep in Bellflower, California.

Don-A-Vee are one of the nation's largest Jeep dealers and keen supporters of Jeep off-road racing and recreational use. Bob's aim with his new Wrangler was to build the 'ideal off-roader' but not interfere with its on-road capabilities. He mixed in suspension, drivetrain, tyre, body, safety and comfort changes to build his dream. Following these photos you'll see what he has done to create his ideal back country Wrangler.

Above

Bob Dibble based his ideal trail Jeep on the brand new 1993 Jeep Wrangler he had purchased from Don-A-Vee Jeep in Bellflower, California. It is all white with the optional composite plastic hardtop and full fender flare kit with step rocker panel. Powering the Jeep is the factory 4.0 litre in-line 'Power-Tech Six' engine which has been upgraded with Borla stainless steel headers and exhaust, Jacobs electronic ignition and a K&N air cleaner. He has also added a 125 psi air compressor under the hood which allows him to quickly change tyre pressure to suit off-road conditions and even repair a tyre in the scrub, should it become necessary.

Above

In its basic form this Wrangler looked like thousands of other Wranglers. Now it's a custom set-up. It was originally quite capable of going down many tough back-country trails. The optional hardtop provides full weather protection and keeps the interior secure and warm. Underneath, Bob had MIT in San Diego, California rework his NP231 transfer case to use 'slip-yoke' drive shafts which offers better off-road reliability than stock when the body is lifted and rougher country tackled.

Right

Bob started on the suspension first. He wanted more ground clearance for the underbelly and the body. He achieved this by installing these 1-inch Currie lift shackles which have grease nipples for lubrication and a set of Superlift 3½-inch Wrangler lift springs which combine to lift the vehicle 4½ inches. This raising of the body allows the Wrangler a tighter approach and departure angle in rough terrain.

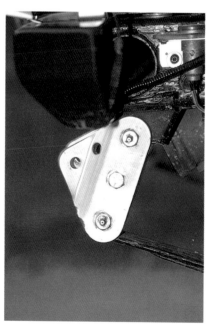

Left

Bob then installed a set of remotely adjustable Rancho RS9000 air shocks which can be adjusted from the driver's seat. This allows him to rapidly change the shock rate depending upon the kind of country he is traversing and to get the ride comfort he wants on the highway.

Below

To improve the traction potential of the Wrangler, Bob dramatically changed the differential assemblies. The rear is now set up with an AMC 20 axle running 4.11 gears, Summers Brothers forged axles and an ARB Air Locker differential which allows him to lock both wheels to get full traction. Up front, Bob retained the Dana 20 but installed a 4.11 gear set and a matching ARB Air Locker for maximum traction. With the two locker axles, Bob can spread the power evenly to all four wheels no matter how bad the traction conditions, allowing the Wrangler to extricate itself from the trickiest situations. Bob also installed a 'Go Rhino' axle skidplate from Off-Road Performance to the front axle for added strength and protection.

Above

To go with the new suspension and drive-train, Bob fitted a set of good-looking
Mickey Thompson/Alcoa forged aluminum wheels which have more than double the
strength of production steel wheels. Bob capped these with 15x8-inch rims with
33x12.5 BF Goodrich Radial All-Terrain T/A tyres. He selected these for their excel-
lent off-road traction and tough sidewall construction. They also add to the height of
the Wrangler and provide good black-top performance.

Right

At the rear Bob installed a Canyon City Swing-Away spare tyre and gas can rack.
Because of the small cargo space inside the Wrangler, rear carry racks are popular
with off-roaders and this is only one of the many styles in use. (See others in the
Jamboree section, pages 105-110.) Bob also installed a Curie Enterprises rear
bumper and tow hitch assembly.

Above

A Warn M8000 power winch is mounted in front of the radiator between the chassis rails. The winch body is covered with a water and dust shield. The winch is set over a Currie rectangular steel bumper which mounts a pair of extra large tow hooks and Hella Rallye 2000 off-road driving lights.

Right

Because of the long distances Bob drives and the rough back country he likes to explore, he upgraded the interior with a pair of Recaro SE sports seats, added a centre console to keep personal items and maps secure, a Cobra HH70 CB radio for safety and a set of Masterac and Tuffy Products storage bins in the rear.

Jeep Racing

The history of Jeep racing goes back to their earliest times when soldiers went messing about with them during the Second World War. Wally Parks, the founder and current president of the National Hot Rod Association (NHRA), recalled during a recent interview that he built several Ford flathead V8-powered Jeeps during his time in the Pacific Islands. These were probably the first hot-rodded Jeeps and apparently used for a little island racing until they were commandeered by senior officers, who also wanted more power than the 'Go-Devil' four-banger offered.

The sixties boom in drag racing produced many kinds of deviations, from go karts to Top Fuel dragsters and Jeeps are part of this story too. In the mid-sixties three Jeeps were top drag racing attractions across the country.

Ed Lenarth's famous *Holy Toledo* drew its name from the city where Jeeps are still built; Roger Wolford in *Secret Weapon*, and the most famous drag racing Jeep of all time, Gene Conway's *The Destroyer*.

Mostly these Jeeps were little more than all-out Fuel Altered class drag racing machines. They were so successful that in 1968 the NHRA banned the body style under pressure from Ford who claimed they couldn't compete with the Jeeps.

When Baja Mexico opened up for racing in the mid-sixties it was the place to go racing with Jeeps. From the first event Jeeps raced there and today Jeeps are still racing in the Baja 1000 race which now uses either a single 500-mile loop circumnavigated twice in the lower Baja Peninsula or the old full peninsula course. In the seventies and eighties CJs and J-series pickups were driven with great success by Don Adams, Bob Gary, Jason Myers and Larry Olson in such races as the Baja 1000, Baja 500, Nevada 500 and Mint 400 desert races.

Mud bog racing also took off in the early eighties and created a following of its own. Privateer Jeep owners built specially powered and modified Jeeps for this new form of motorsport. Mud bog racing started out in the south and developed into a professional touring circuit appearing at fairgrounds and stadiums.

Off-road racing has been very popular with competitors for years. This Wrangler raced by the team of Don Adams and Larry Olsen is sponsored by beer brewer, Stroh, and the Imperial Palace Casino in Las Vegas. The roof-mounted wing is designed to add stability to the Wrangler at high speed and all the lights help the racers find their way through the desert night, where the racers have no marked roads, only tracks to follow. (Pete Biro)

In the mid-eighties, Jeep supported six factory racing Jeeps with stunning success. Under the leadership and driving skills of the Archer Brothers, Jeep won the 1987 Manufacturers Championship in the 'Racetruck Challenge' run by the Sports Car Club of America (SCCA) driving a Comanche pickup.

In the Desert Racing Series run by HDRA/SCORE, Mike Lesle (*sic*) won the championship in 1987 and by the end of the decade Jeep had picked off another four manufacturer championships.

Racing into the nineties, the new Mickey Thompson Stadium Racing series has brought off-road racing to the public in their own back yard. Mike Lesle Racing-Jeep Motorsports Team put a four Cherokee team to work in 1992 producing six different championship wins in both Stadium and SCORE/HDRA Desert Off-Road racing.

Ed Lenarth's Holy Toledo *Funny Car Jeep drag racer was one of three Jeep-bodied Funny Cars raced in the late sixties and early seventies. The NHRA outlawed the second generation Lenarth Jeep along with the other Jeeps including Gene Conway's* The Destroyer. *These Jeeps were extremely fast and turned speeds of over 200 mph in the quarter mile. (Steve Reyes)*

Above

Mud bog racing became popular in the early eighties around the country. Promoters worked the new sport something like an old-time circus show, moving from one town to the next, setting up shows with man-made mud-bogs at fairgrounds and stadiums for weekend events. The shows mixed professional mud bog racers with local heroes who would compete for cash awards or just the glory of making it through the mud bog. This modified early CJ-5 featured V8 power, a full roll-cage and 'mud-paddle' flotation tyres.

Left

Jeep Cherokees are also a very popular racing class. This Craftsman Tools-sponsored two-door wagon flies through the air in the Mint Casino-sponsored off-road race with Evan Evans at the wheel. The huge wheels and 20 inches of wheel travel allow this racing Jeep to leap over many rock ridges that production Cherokees would need to crawl across. (Pete Biro)

Above

The Sports Car Club of America (SCCA) developed a sport truck racing series in the mid-eighties called the 'Racetruck Challenge'. All the major compact and mid-sized truck manufacturers entered teams and raced in the series. Here a Ford Ranger and one of Archer Brothers Jeep Comanche pickups 'duel' into the braking zone at the bottom turn on Sears Point International Raceway in Sonoma County, California, during the first race. The Archer Brothers Jeep Comanche eventually won the 1987 Manufacturers Championship in the 'Racetruck Challenge'.

Left

As you can see from this photo, the wheels on this Randall Racing Jeep Comanche pickup truck have an enormous amount of travel which allows them to flex and move over the terrain as the truck thunders down the off-road course. One spare tyre is mounted on a rack in the back in case of a flat while out on the course. (Pete Biro)

Above

This virtually stock 1993 six-cylinder Jeep Grand Cherokee was driven in the 1992 Paris-Moscow-Beijing Rally. It was the first such rally since a similar race in 1907. The racers used this new Grand Cherokee which had just been released in late 1992 as the 1993 model. The 10,000 mile rally was driven by two journalists, Chris Jensen and Phil Berg, along with veteran rally driver Bryant Hibbs.

Right

Mike Lesle's Racing Jeep Cherokee is seen here going full bore in a recent off-road race in Nevada. Mike has run multi-car teams with Curt LeDuc, Steve Kelly, Tommy Croft, Larry Noel and himself as drivers in both SCORE International and HDRA events. Mike has also raced a team of Jeeps in the Mickey Thompson Stadium series where they have been one of the winningest teams of all time. In the past four years the team has won with Jeeps an amazing six championships in both Stadium and Desert Off-Road racing. This 500 hp racer is completely hand-fabricated with tubular frame and trick suspension designed for the ruggedness of off-road racing. (Pete Biro)

JEEP tours take you off the beaten path.

Courtesy of the cities of Phoenix, Mesa, Scottsdale and Tempe, Arizona. For visitor information write to: Phoenix Convention and Visitors Bureau, One, Arizona Center, 400 E, Van Buren Street, Suite 600, Phoenix, Arizona, 85004-2290.